CHARMAINE SOLOMON
WOK
COOKBOOK

CHARMAINE SOLOMON
WOK
COOKBOOK

Text and recipes by
CHARMAINE SOLOMON

Photography by
REG MORRISON

CRESCENT BOOKS
New York

ACKNOWLEDGEMENTS

I should like to acknowledge the assistance of Cathay Pacific Airways Ltd; Mr Peter Liu, Liu Rose Restaurant, Concord Rd, North Strathfield, N.S.W.; Asia Provisions Pty Limited, Victoria Ave, Chatswood, N.S.W.; Ward's Stoves Manufacturing Pty Limited, Fred St, Leichhardt, N.S.W.; Cook-On Gas Products, Gibb St, Chatswood, N.S.W.; Rinnai Australia Pty Ltd; Monier Metal Products; Alan Hardy of the Committee of Direction of Fruit Marketing; and John Miller of the Australian Mushroom Growers' Association.

First published 1979
© Copyright RPLA Pty Limited 1979
This edition is published by Crescent Books,
distributed by Crown Publishers, Inc.
  h g f e d e b
1981 EDITION
Second impression 1982

Printed in Hong Kong
by South China Printing Co.

Library of Congress Cataloging in Publication Data

Solomon, Charmaine.
  Wok cookbook

  Includes index.
  1. Wok cookery. I. Title.
TX840.W65S64 1981   641.5'8   81-17249
ISBN 0-517-37100-6   AACR2

Page 1: Master Chef Peter Liu with woks and other equipment of a Chinese kitchen.
Page 2: Fried Pork and Crab Rolls, recipe page 23.

PREFACE

Fast, efficient, versatile: these three words sum up the wok as a cooking utensil. The wok has been used in China for hundreds of years, but a look at what's happening in Australia and America shows that it's the 'in' thing to own and use a wok. Real wok enthusiasts have several, and in varying sizes.

And why not? The wok can do anything that's asked of it. It is the most efficient single utensil there is, and that's the truth, considering that in a wok you can boil, braise, steam, simmer, deep fry, shallow fry and stir fry, proving its versatility over any other pot. Deep frying requires much less oil because of the curved shape. With the addition of a high domed lid you can stew or braise a whole duck or chicken. With a steamer tray and lid you can steam anything from fish, poultry and pork to a delectable savarin for dessert!

But it is in stir frying, the most commonly used technique in Chinese cooking, that the wok really comes into its own. The thin metal heats up quickly and its flaring sides allow you to toss and stir with abandon so that all the food comes into contact with the heat yet doesn't get tossed all over the stove or the floor, all too easily done when using a conventional frying pan.

Remember the trouble Aladdin's wife got into when she succumbed to the temptation of exchanging an old lamp for a new one? Washing and drying my woks, I've often thought how unwilling I would be to exchange these blackened pans for even the shiniest, most expensive new wok I could be offered. For there's something that happens to a wok after long and loving use. It takes on what the Chinese call 'Wok Hay' — a sort of character of its own. They swear food tastes better cooked in an old wok, a veteran of many meals.

Indeed, there's something almost as magical about a wok as there was about Aladdin's wonderful lamp. He used to give it a rub and wish he were in a distant land and presto, he was! It takes just a little longer with a wok, but you can cook yourself into any country you desire . . . for though the wok is a Chinese utensil, it cooks in any language.

Throughout the lands of Asia one finds the same curved, deeply sloping pan — the Malaysian kuwali, the Indonesian wadjan, the Philippine carajay, the Indian karahi. They do the same variety of jobs.

The idea behind wok design was to conserve fuel, for this has always been in extremely short supply in the crowded land of China. The food is cut into bite-size pieces in such a way that the greatest surface area is presented to the heat. A quick stir fry on high heat and the dish is ready to eat in less than 5 minutes. Set the table before you start to cook, for you won't have time while the food cooks, it all happens so fast. As soon as it is ready this type of dish should be served, so it doesn't continue to cook in its own heat, or vegetables will not be so crisp, meats so juicy.

Wok enthusiasts usually start cooking in the wok because they like Chinese food but soon find they can use the wok for just about anything . . . Beef Stroganoff, Italian-style tripe, Provincial French ratatouille. This old Chinese invention is right for today's needs in the kitchen, where most people are adventuring with food from other lands.

As nobody can improve on the design of the wok, it hasn't been changed in centuries. It holds in goodness and flavour because of the quick, high heat, so food is more nutritious. In short, the wok is a great international cooking pot, even if the Chinese did think of it first.

CONTENTS

MEAT 71

INTRODUCTION

BUYING A WOK

Don't assume that the most expensive wok must necessarily be the best one! My favourite 'old faithful' is ordinary rolled steel and was purchased relatively cheaply. It has been used almost daily for many years and seems to be all set for many years of faithful service. The thin metal heats up quickly and evenly and with proper care and frequent use the wok will not rust.

The many kinds of woks on the market today show how popular this utensil is becoming. There are stainless steel woks and woks with non-stick linings; woks with flattened base for better contact with electric hotplates and an electric wok with its built-in element that is handsome enough to bring to the table as a serving dish. And you can cook at the table in the electric wok or on a portable gas cooker. (See section on Table-top Cooking.)

Each kind of wok has its advantages and disadvantages. Stainless steel looks beautiful and shiny but the metal is not a good conductor of heat. Although non-stick linings may not stick, food is inclined to burn more easily. The electric wok is much more efficient than a wok used on an electric stove, but follow instructions and do not cook more than the stated quantity of food at a time. Actually this applies to stir frying in any wok, even when cooking by gas but is specially important when cooking by electricity, as it takes time for the heat to build up again when food is added.

When using a wok on an electric cooker, the trick is to make it very hot by using the hotplate on the highest setting, then to move the wok on and off the hotplate as more or less heat is required, since electricity does not have the flexibility of gas.

The perforated metal ring sold as an optional extra is necessary for some stoves and not for others. If your gas stove has the sort of grid arrangement that holds the wok steady, well and good. If, on the other hand, the grid is so designed that the curved base of the wok causes it to wobble unsteadily, buy a ring to make it steady and safe. It may be necessary to lift off the regular grid before putting the ring in place. The perforations on the ring allow ventilation, and the sides slope so that one opening is larger than the other.

The ring has sloping sides for a good reason. When less heat is needed, for example when simmering, the smaller opening should be on top to hold the wok further away from the heat. When more heat is needed, as in a quick stir-fry, the larger opening should be upwards so that the wok is allowed to sit closer to the source of heat.

Always remember the rule, 'hot wok, warm oil' when frying. In other words heat the wok first, then add the oil and allow the oil to heat. It only takes a few seconds, but heating the wok first ensures that the oil spreads more easily and the ingredients will not stick to the pan.

For domestic use, the 30-35 cm (12-14 inch) wok is most useful, even if you are cooking for only one or two people. Remember you can cook small quantities in a large wok but not large quantities in a small wok. Besides, when it comes to stir frying you need room for that tossing of ingredients and a wok that is too small definitely cramps one's style. The metal should be thin, but not too thin. A 14-inch wok should weigh about 1 kg.

PREPARING A WOK FOR USE

A stainless steel, aluminium or electric wok needs only to be washed with hot water and detergent to rid it of dust, industrial grime and machine oil. But a rolled steel wok needs more attention. Since this metal rusts, manuacturers give it a coating of oil. Sometimes this yields to a good soaking in hot soapy water but occasionally it is stubborn, and needs to be removed by filling the wok with water, adding about 2 tablespoons of bicarbonate of soda and boiling for 15 minutes. This softens the coating and it can be scrubbed off with a fine scourer. If necessary, repeat the process until the wok is free from any coating on the inside.

The wok must now be seasoned. To season a new wok, rinse and dry it well, put over gentle heat and, when the metal heats up, wipe over the entire inner surface with a wad of absorbent kitchen paper dipped in peanut oil. Repeat a number of times with paper and oil. At first the paper will come away looking a rusty brown, but after a few times the paper remains clean. Allow wok to cool. It is now ready for use.

After cooking in the wok, do not scrub with steel wool or abrasives of any kind. If food sticks, soak in hot water to soften food, then rub gently with a sponge or dish mop or one of the bamboo wok scrubbers, using hot water and detergent. Dry the wok well and heat it gently to make sure it is quite dry, because any moisture left in the wok will cause it to rust. Rub over the inner surface with a lightly oiled paper.

A well seasoned wok will turn black, but this is normal and the more a wok is used, the better it is to cook in.

The two metal handles on either side of the wok get quite hot as cooking progresses, so always have a pot holder ready. The professional Chinese chefs always use a damp kitchen towel, folded so that its many thicknesses keep the user from buring his fingers. Being somewhat forgetful about such things, I have found that three or four layers of insulating tape wound around the handles prevents many a blister, but after a while the tape becomes tacky and has to be removed and replaced with fresh tape.

There are some woks available with a long wooden handle, much easier to use if you've been accustomed to Western-style pans or skillets.

Hang your wok over the stove or somewhere within easy reach so you can use it often. Another reason it is better to hang it or store it on an open shelf is that the oil which protects it from rust will go rancid in a dark, warm place.

Anyway, once you find how easy to use and versatile the wok is, you'll be reaching for it every day and it does look picturesque in a kitchen.

OTHER EQUIPMENT

When you buy a wok, buy a lid for it too, because it is necessary when braising or steaming. Aluminium lids with heatproof handles are usually sold wherever woks are sold, and if you have a choice of shape choose a high-domed lid rather than a gently curved one because this enables you to cook a whole chicken or duck. But more important than the height of the lid is the edge. See that it fits well and makes contact with the wok all round so that heat is not dissipated. Treat it with care too for if it is dropped from a height the thin metal will warp and let the heat escape.

A bamboo steamer is another great piece of equipment to have and again it is decorative enough to hang on the wall or leave on an open shelf. It is particularly suitable for steaming buns or dumplings or cakes or desserts, as excess steam does not gather on the inside of the lid and fall back on the delicate goodies, spotting them with moisture. Steamers are sold in sets of 2 tiers and 1 lid and the most popular sizes are 26 and 30 cm (10½ and 12 inches). My steamer is the 45 cm (15-inch) size and in it I steam main dishes, dim sum, pork buns, black bean buns, caramel custards and even desserts like the delectable savarin pictured on page 112.

If you don't have a bamboo steamer, you can improvise a steamer by putting a perforated disc or metal rack in the wok to hold the food above the level of the water. The food is put on a plate of a size that will allow free circulation of steam around it, and the wok covered with a well fitting lid. If you don't want moisture to drop into a particular dish, cover the plate of food loosely with foil.

For transferring food from the wok you will need a ladle and a perforated spoon. While the Chinese wok chan and wire frying spoons are very attractive and efficient, most slotted spoons will do the job. (I'm very partial to a cheap, easily obtainable curved slotted utensil which has just the right shape for the wok and is not as noisy as a wok chan.)

Some woks with special coatings need utensils that won't scratch the lining of the metal. In this case wood or heat-proof plastic utensils are required, whilst a pair of long wooden cooking chopsticks is also useful, as are tongs.

If you do much deep frying, a metal bowl large enough to pour oil into is an asset, and for draining deep fried food, Chinese chefs usually rest a wire straining spoon on the bowl and tip the contents of the wok into the bowl. The oil goes through, and the food is drained.

WHAT TO COOK ON

For wok cookery, gas is a natural. With some of the modern gas cooktops, for example those that have four staggered burners, you can accommodate two woks at the same time, one at either end, perhaps braising or steaming in one and making a stir-fried dish in the other. When you get really proficient, you will be able to make two stir-fried dishes at once, which needs at bit of concentration but is quite fun to do and most impressive to watch. The secret, as when making any stir-fried dish, is to have everything cut up, measured and ready and just add to the wok in the correct order.

For those who are really serious about wok cookery, and especially about Chinese-style food, there are a number of choices in wok cookers. The most impressive and efficient of these is the Ward's Wok Stove which can be connected to mains gas or operates with a cylinder. It is of stainless steel, has a double ring for fast cooking when it is required, and takes any size wok. It supplies 40,000 B.T.U's and the normal domestic range supplies 8,000, so that will give you some idea of the difference. Ward's make and supply wok stoves to Chinese restaurants, but also supply a domestic model, single-burner size.

Then there is the more modestly priced Rinnai wok cooker (16,000 B.T.U's) which has four heat settings. It is available to suit mains gas or L.P.G. When used with a gas cylinder it is ideal for outdoor cooking but it is also particularly suitable for cooking on at the table. This too is made in Australia.

Portable gas rings marketed in Australia by Cook On Gas Products, Chatswood, N.S.W., are most convenient for table-top cooking, outdoor use, or simply to augment your cooking facilities if your kitchen is all electric and you want to get best results with the wok. These are used with gas cylinders and are available in three models.

The controls enable the larger rings to be used either singly or in combination. A single ring supplies 25,000 B.T.U's, a dual ring 36,000 B.T.U's, and a triple ring 40,000 B.T.U.'s.

The electric Wonder Wok made by Monier has a thermostat for controlling the exact degree of heat required. It comes complete with utensils recommended for use with the wok so that its anodised inner surface remains undamaged, and has a draining rack with clips on the side of the wok for deep fried foods. It has a heatproof base and may be placed directly on the table. The outer finish is in a warm red.

WOK
TECHNIQUE

Using a wok is not difficult. Just make sure, as described on page 11, that the wok sits securely and steadily on the stove with no danger of tipping over. Use the metal ring if necessary to ensure stability.

All the cooking techniques you use in Western cooking are possible in a wok. The advantage of the wok over other utensils is that it has no corners. Its open shape also means that when cooking a whole chicken or duck or a large cauliflower, it is easier to lift it out of the wok than out of a straight-sided pan. Another plus — when frying, the amount of oil needed is much less because of the wok's curved shape.

The only point to watch is that, when simmering or braising, the heat is carefully controlled. Being of thin metal, cooking takes place more quickly than in conventional utensils, so stir from time to time and ensure there is enough liquid to prevent burning.

A little concentration the first few times you use a wok will help you appreciate the new shorter timing required and after you become accustomed to it, you will be impatient when you use a conventional pan.

There is actually only one wok technique that is different from any of those used in Western cookery, and that is stir frying. This is the method used for those short-cooked Oriental dishes that appear as if by magic. If you have visited Asian cities and been to the roadside food stalls where your meal is put before you less than 5 minutes from the time you order, you know how impressive it is. Since it is usually cooked right in front of you, you also have a good idea of what is meant by the 'stir' part of stir frying. If you have not seen this being done, I must emphasise that it is not the circular motion indicated by the word 'stir' in Western cooking, the spoon moving round and around in the same direction.

It is something much more spectacular and unrestrained. It takes in tossing, flipping, turning over, everything kept moving at speed so that all the surfaces of the food come into contact with the hot wok and the small amount of oil used for cooking in this manner.

The essence of stir frying is split-second timing, so when making a stir-fried dish every bit of preparation must be completed before cooking starts. The ingredients must be sliced, diced, marinated or whatever the recipe calls for. The seasonings should all be measured out and at hand.

Read the recipe carefully and arrange everything in the order in which it will be needed. Once you start to cook there's no stopping to find a dash of this or that — you'll interrupt the rhythm of the cooking. Ingredients are added in a pre-arranged order, those which take longest to cook going into the wok first and others following at intervals so that they are all ready at the same time. The method may seem difficult at first, but study a recipe and you will realise how logical it is.

Once you actually cook a stir-fried dish (having properly organised your ingredients beforehand) you will become addicted, as I have, to this method of cooking — it's so wonderfully quick and besides, the results are delicious.

Remember to heat the wok before adding the oil. Then pick up the wok by the handles and swirl to coat with oil before adding ingredients. Since so little oil is used in stir frying, this ensures it is spread over the inner surface so ingredients won't stick.

Stir-fried dishes must be served immediately they are ready or they will continue to cook in their own heat, losing the crisp texture and the special flavour that comes from the fierce heat and short cooking time. So before you start to cook have serving plate heated and ready, guests hungry and waiting, and let no time be lost in serving and eating. *Bon appetit!*

GUIDE TO WEIGHTS AND MEASURES

The metric weights and metric fluid measures used in this book are those of the *Standards Association of Australia*. A good set of scales, a graduated Australian Standard measuring cup and a set of Australian measuring spoons will be very helpful and can be obtained from leading hardware and kitchenware stores.

All cup and spoon measurements are level:

- The *Australian Standard measuring cup* has a capacity of 250 millilitres (250 ml).
- The *Australian Standard tablespoon* has a capacity of 20 millilitres (20 ml).
- The *Australian Standard teaspoon* has a capacity of 5 millilitres (5 ml).

In all recipes, imperial equivalents of metric measures are shown in parentheses, e.g. 500 g (1 lb) beef. Although the metric yields of cup and weighed measures are approximately 10 per cent greater than the imperial yields, the proportions remain the same. Therefore, for successful cooking use either metric or imperial weights and measures — do not mix the two.

New Zealand, British, United States and Canadian weights and measures are the same as Australian weights and measures except that:

(a) the Australian and British Standard tablespoons have a capacity of 20 millilitres (20 ml) whereas the New Zealand, United States and Canadian Standard tablespoons have a capacity of 15 millilitres (15 ml), therefore all tablespoon measures should be taken generously in those countries;
(b) the imperial pint (Australia, New Zealand and Britain) has a capacity of 20 fl oz whereas the US pint used in the United States and Canada has a capacity of 16 fl oz, therefore pint measures should be increased accordingly in those two countries.

The following charts of conversion equivalents will be useful:

Imperial Weight	Metric Weight
½ oz	15 g
1 oz	30 g
2 oz	60 g
3 oz	90 g
4 oz (¼ lb)	125 g
6 oz	185 g
8 oz (½ lb)	250 g
12 oz (¾ lb)	375 g
16 oz (1 lb)	500 g
24 oz (1½ lb)	750 g
32 oz (2 lb)	1000 g (1 kg)
3 lb	1500 g (1.5 kg)
4 lb	2000 g (2 kg)

Key: oz = ounce; lb = pound; g = gram; kg = kilogram.

Imperial Liquid Measures	Cup Measures	Metric Liquid Measures
1 fl oz		30 ml
2 fl oz	¼ cup	
3 fl oz		100 ml
4 fl oz (¼ pint US)	½ cup	
5 fl oz (¼ pint imp.)		150 ml
6 fl oz	¾ cup	
8 fl oz (½ pint US)	1 cup	250 ml
10 fl oz (½ pint imp.)	1¼ cups	
12 fl oz	1½ cups	
14 fl oz	1¾ cups	
16 fl oz (1 pint US)	2 cups	500 ml
20 fl oz (1 pint imp.)	2½ cups	

Key: fl oz = fluid ounce; ml = millilitre.

Opposite: Fried Camembert and Savoury Cheese Bites, recipes page 22.

THE
RECIPES
INTERNATIONAL COOKING
WITH A WOK

Opposite: Steamed Pearl Balls, recipe page 23.

APPETISERS

FRIED CAMEMBERT

ENGLAND DENMARK

*Each small camembert will serve 8. Cook just
before serving.*

See picture page 19

1 small ripe camembert, well chilled
1 egg, beaten
dry breadcrumbs or cornflake
   crumbs
oil for deep frying

Cut the cheese into 8 equal wedges. Dip in beaten egg, then into crumbs
and make sure that cheese is coated all over. If preferred, this may be done
beforehand and the cheese returned to the refrigerator until serving time.
   Heat oil in wok until hot but not smoking. Fry the cheese just until
golden, drain on absorbent paper and serve quickly. The frying should not
take more than 2 or 3 minutes. The crust should be crisp and the cheese
soft and melting. Hand small paper napkins with the cheese.

SAVOURY CHEESE BITES

ENGLAND

Makes about 2 dozen

See picture page 19

¾ cup finely grated natural cheddar
1½ cups soft white breadcrumbs
2 eggs, beaten
salt and pepper to taste
2 teaspoons prepared mustard
dry breadcrumbs
oil for deep frying

Combine cheese and breadcrumbs in a bowl. Beat the eggs until frothy and
mix in the salt, pepper and mustard. Combine with the cheese mixture and
form into small balls. If mixture is too moist add a little more soft
breadcrumbs, but do not make the texture too dry and crumbly. Roll the
balls in dry breadcrumbs to coat.
   Heat oil for deep frying in wok and when hot, fry a few of the cheese
balls at a time on medium heat until they are golden brown all over. Lift out
on slotted spoon and drain on absorbent paper. Serve warm or cold.

22

STEAMED PEARL BALLS CHINA

Serves: 4-6

See picture page 20

1 cup short grain rice
8 dried Chinese mushrooms
250 g (8 oz) minced lean topside
250 g (8 oz) minced pork
4 spring onions, finely chopped
1 teaspoon finely grated fresh ginger
½ teaspoon crushed garlic
1 teaspoon salt
¼ teaspoon ground black pepper
1 tablespoon light soy sauce
1 egg, beaten
¼ cup finely chopped water
  chestnuts

Soak rice in cold water to cover for at least 2 hours, then drain well, spread on kitchen paper and leave to dry while preparing meat balls. Soak mushrooms in hot water for 30 minutes. Squeeze out excess water, discard stems and chop caps finely. Put into a large bowl with all the remaining ingredients and mix very well with the hands. Shape into balls about 2.5 cm (1 inch) in diameter, rolling them between your palms. Roll each ball separately in the rice with enough pressure to make the rice stick and coat the ball.

Oil a steamer rack and put the balls on it, leaving space between so the rice can swell as it steams. Fill wok with water up to 2.5 cm (1 inch) below rack, bring water to the boil and steam the pearl balls, covered, for 40 minutes. If necessary add more boiling water to wok.

The rice will swell and the balls will be covered with pearly grains when done.

FRIED PORK AND CRAB ROLLS VIETNAM

Makes about 24

See picture page 2

½ cup soaked cellophane noodles
1 small onion, finely chopped
6 spring onions, finely chopped
250 g (8 oz) pork mince
185 g (6 oz) crab meat, frozen or
  canned
½ teaspoon salt
1 tablespoon fish sauce
¼ teaspoon ground black pepper
half packet Chinese spring roll
  pastry
oil for deep frying

For Serving:
lettuce leaves
sprigs of mint and fresh coriander
cucumber cut in julienne strips

Soak a small amount of cellophane noodles in hot water for 10 minutes, then drain and measure ½ cup. Roughly chop and put into a bowl with the onion, spring onion, pork, flaked crab meat, salt, fish sauce and pepper. Mix well. Cut each spring roll wrapper in halves and put 2 teaspoons of filling on one end, shaping it into a neat roll. Roll up, turning in the sides so that the filling is completely enclosed. Moisten edge of wrapper with a little water or egg white to stick. When all the rolls are made, heat oil in a wok and fry a few at a time on medium heat until they are crisp and golden. Do not have oil too hot or the filling will not cook through. Drain on kitchen paper.

To serve: Wrap each roll in a lettuce leaf including a sprig of mint, some fresh coriander and a strip of cucumber. Dip in nuoc cham sauce and eat immediately.

Nuoc cham sauce: Combine 1 teaspoon crushed garlic with 1 tablespoon chilli sauce, 1 teaspoon sugar, 1 tablespoon lemon juice, 1 tablespoon vinegar, 1 tablespoon water and 4 tablespoons fish sauce.

PRAWN FRITTERS

INDONESIA

Makes approx. 18

250 g (8 oz) shelled raw prawns
2 eggs, beaten
1 tablespoon water
1 tablespoon rice flour
2 tablespoons ground rice
½ teaspoon crushed garlic
¾ teaspoon salt
¼ teaspoon ground black pepper
¼ teaspoon kencur powder, optional
¼ teaspoon sereh powder, optional
1 fresh red chilli, seeded and sliced
1 small onion, quartered and sliced
peanut oil for deep frying

De-vein prawns and chop. Mix together the eggs, water, rice flour, ground rice, garlic, salt, pepper and other spices. Fold in the chilli, onion and prawns.

Heat oil in wok and when very hot drop batter by scant tablespoons into the oil, 3 or 4 at a time. Fry over medium heat until golden brown on both sides, drain on absorbent paper and serve hot.

PRAWN CUTLETS

CHINA

Serves: 4-6

12 raw king prawns
2 tablespoons soy sauce
1 small clove garlic, crushed
¼ teaspoon salt
½ teaspoon finely grated fresh ginger
½ cup cornflour
1 large egg, beaten
dry breadcrumbs or cornflake
   crumbs
peanut oil for deep frying
lemon wedges for serving
chilli sauce for dipping, optional

Shell and de-vein prawns, leaving last segment of shell and the tail on. With a sharp knife slit prawns along curve of back but do not cut right through. Combine soy sauce, garlic, salt and ginger together and marinate prawns in this mixture for 15 minutes or longer.

Dip prawns into cornflour, shake off excess, then dip in beaten egg and finally into crumbs, pressing gently to flatten prawns and firm the coating.

Heat oil in wok until almost smoking. Fry a few prawns at a time until golden brown, about 2 or 3 minutes. Drain on absorbent paper and serve hot with lemon wedges. Serve chilli sauce for dipping if liked.

COCONUT AND BEEF CROQUETTES

INDONESIA

Makes 50-60 cocktail size meatballs

250 g (8 oz) desiccated coconut
about ½ cup hot water
500 g (1 lb) hamburger mince
½ teaspoon dried shrimp paste
2 cloves garlic
1½ teaspoons salt
½ teaspoon ground black pepper
1½ teaspoons ground coriander
1 teaspoon ground cummin
½ teaspoon ground kencur (aromatic
**   ginger)**
2 eggs, beaten
peanut oil for deep frying

Put coconut into a bowl and sprinkle with the hot water. Mix until all the coconut is moistened. Combine coconut and hamburger mince.

In a small bowl crush shrimp paste with back of spoon and dissolve in a tablespoon of hot water. Crush garlic with salt. Add to shrimp paste together with black pepper and all the spices, add beaten eggs and mix well. Pour over the meat and coconut, mix and knead well with the hands so that spices are evenly distributed and mixture is smooth. Shape into small balls. Deep fry in hot oil until they are crisp and golden brown all over. Drain on absorbent paper and serve warm or cold.

These meatballs may be served as appetisers or as an accompaniment to a meal of rice and curry.

SESAME PRAWN TOAST

CHINA

Serve as an appetiser, or as a cocktail savoury
Makes about 24 pieces

250 g (8 oz) raw prawns (in shells)
1 tablespoon beaten egg
½ teaspoon finely grated fresh ginger
½ teaspoon salt
1 tablespoon oyster sauce
2 teaspoons cornflour
6 slices white bread
¾ cup sesame seeds
oil for deep frying

Shell and de-vein prawns. If using frozen peeled raw prawns, thaw completely and drain off liquid, then weigh 125 g (4 oz). Chop prawns very finely and mix with the beaten egg, ginger, salt, oyster sauce and cornflour. Trim crusts off bread and spread the slices with the prawn mixture. Toast the sesame seeds in wok over low heat, stirring constantly and taking care that seeds do not burn. As soon as they are golden, turn on to a plate.

Wipe out wok with paper and heat oil for deep frying. Dip slices of bread in the sesame seeds, pressing the prawn mixture firmly on the seeds. Put the bread on a wooden board and use a sharp knife or chopper to cut each slice into 4 narrow strips. Fry the strips, not too many at once, in hot oil until the bread is golden brown. Drain on absorbent paper and serve hot.

STEAMED SAUSAGE BUNS

CHINA

Makes 12 buns

185 g (6 oz) Chinese pork sausages (lap cheong)
4 dried Chinese mushrooms
2 teaspoons peanut oil
½ teaspoon finely chopped garlic
¼ teaspoon salt
½ cup hot water
1 canned bamboo shoot, finely chopped
1 tablespoon dark soy sauce
1 teaspoon sesame oil
2 teaspoons oyster sauce
1 tablespoon cornflour
2 teaspoons hoi sin sauce
2 teaspoons sugar
1 quantity bun dough (see page 119)

Steam sausages for 15 minutes, cool and thinly slice diagonally. Soak Chinese mushrooms in hot water for 30 minutes, squeeze out excess water, discard stems and slice caps finely. Heat oil in a wok, add garlic and cook very slowly, not allowing garlic to brown. Add salt, hot water, mushrooms, bamboo shoot, soy sauce, sesame oil and oyster sauce. Mix cornflour with a tablespoon of cold water and stir in, then cook stirring until thick and clear. Remove from heat, stir in hoi sin sauce and sugar. Cool, then stir in sliced pork sausages. Mould and steam buns as described below.

Bun dough: To make buns, divide dough into 12 portions and mould each into a smooth ball. Roll out on a very lightly floured board to a circle about 10 cm (4 inches) across. Put a tablespoon of filling in centre of circle and gather sides together, folding and pleating to make a neat join. Twist dough to seal. Put each bun, join downwards, on a square of greaseproof paper lightly brushed with sesame oil. Put in bamboo steamer, cover and steam for 20 minutes. Serve warm. The cooked buns can be refrigerated overnight and reheated by steaming for 3 minutes before serving.

Note: If using a metal steamer, put a clean tea towel across steaming tray before covering with lid to prevent condensation dropping on top of buns.

SPRING ROLLS

Yield: 20-24

6 dried Chinese mushrooms
3 tablespoons peanut oil
1 tablespoon sesame oil
½ teaspoon finely chopped garlic
½ teaspoon finely chopped fresh
   ginger
250 g (8 oz) finely minced pork
250 g (8 oz) raw prawns, de-veined
   and chopped
2 cups shredded Chinese cabbage
12 water chestnuts, chopped or
1 cup canned bamboo shoot, chopped
125 g (4 oz) bean sprouts
6 spring onions, finely chopped
1 tablespoon dark soy sauce
1 tablespoon oyster sauce
1 teaspoon salt
3 teaspoons cornflour
1 packet frozen spring roll pastry
oil for deep frying

Cover mushrooms with hot water and soak for 20 minutes. Discard stems and chop mushrooms. Heat peanut and sesame oil in a wok and slowly fry garlic and ginger for a few seconds. Add pork and fry until it changes colour. Add prawns and continue stir frying until they are cooked. Add vegetables, soy sauce, oyster sauce and salt, combine thoroughly. Push mixture to one side and tilt wok so liquid gathers. Stir in cornflour which has been mixed with a little cold water until smooth. Cook, stirring continuously, until thick.

Remove wok from heat and mix thickened liquid through the filling. Allow to cool completely. Place 2 tablespoons of the mixture at one end of each spring roll wrapper and roll up, turning in the sides so that filling is completely enclosed. Dampen edges with water or a mixture of cornflour and water and press to seal. Fry one or two at a time in deep hot oil until golden brown. Drain on kitchen paper and serve immediately, with chilli sauce if desired.

CURRY PUFFS

SRI LANKA

Makes about 75 small puffs

A wok is ideal for all kinds of deep frying, as the shape means you need less oil, and the items are not crowded.

2 tablespoons oil or ghee
1 teaspoon finely chopped garlic
2 teaspoons finely grated fresh ginger
2 large onions, finely chopped
1 tablespoon Ceylon curry powder
1 kg (2 lb) minced meat
2 teaspoons salt
2 tablespoons lemon juice
½ cup hot water
2 potatoes, diced small
6 hard-boiled eggs
oil for deep frying

Pastry:
2 cups plain flour
pinch baking powder
½ teaspoon salt
1 teaspoon caster sugar
125 g (4 oz) butter or margarine
2 tablespoons lemon juice
4-5 tablespoons iced water
1 egg white

Heat oil or ghee in a large, heavy saucepan and fry the garlic, ginger and onions, stirring frequently, until soft and golden. Add the curry powder and fry for a minute longer. Add the meat and fry, stirring constantly, until it has lost its pinkness and no lumps remain. Add the salt, lemon juice, and water, cover and cook on low heat for 15 minutes. Add the potatoes and continue cooking for a further 15 minutes or until potatoes are tender and almost all the liquid is absorbed. Allow to cool, then mix in the chopped hard-boiled eggs.

Pastry: Sift flour, baking powder, salt and sugar into a bowl and rub in the shortening. Mix lemon juice and iced water and add to flour, mixing to a smooth dough. Add a little more water if necessary. Wrap in greaseproof paper and chill for 30 minutes before rolling out.

Roll out a quarter of the pastry at a time on a lightly floured board. It should be very thin, about ⅛ inch. Cut into circles using a large scone cutter 8 cm (3¼ inches) in diameter. Put a teaspoonful of the filling on each pastry round. Wet the edges of the pastry with slightly beaten egg white, fold over to make a half circle and press edges firmly together to seal. Press with a fork or pastry cutter to make a decorative edge.

When all the curry puffs are made, fry a few at a time in deep, hot vegetable oil. Drain on absorbent paper and serve warm, or prepare ahead and heat in a moderately hot oven before serving.

STEAMED PRAWN DUMPLINGS   CHINA

Makes about 24

Called siew mai by the Chinese, these are known as dim sims among Westerners.

500 g (1 lb) small raw prawns
6 dried Chinese mushrooms
6 canned water chestnuts, chopped
  finely
3 tablespoons finely chopped bamboo
  shoot
3 spring onions, chopped
250 g (8 oz) minced pork
1½ teaspoons salt
1 tablespoon light soy sauce
1 tablespoon Chinese wine or dry
  sherry
1 teaspoon sesame oil
1 egg white
125 g (4 oz) wonton wrappers

Peel prawns, reserve about 24 for garnish and chop the remaining prawns. Soak mushrooms in hot water 30 minutes, then slice off and discard stems. Chop mushroom caps. Combine all chopped ingredients with pork, salt, soy sauce, wine, sesame oil and egg white. Mix well together and put 1 heaped teaspoon of mixture in the centre of each wonton wrapper. Gather the wrapper around filling and press it close to give the shape of a little money bag, open at the top. Press a prawn on top of each for garnish.

Lightly oil a steamer tray and put siew mai in a single layer on the tray. Pour enough water into a wok to come just below the level of the steaming basket. Cover with lid and steam over boiling water for 20 minutes. Serve hot or cold.

SPLIT PEA AND ONION FRITTERS   BURMA

Serves: 6-8

A favourite snack in Burma, similar to those vegetable fritters known as pakorhas in India.

1 cup split peas
2 medium onions, finely chopped
2 fresh red chillies, finely chopped or
  ¼ teaspoon chilli powder
½ teaspoon ground turmeric
½ teaspoon salt
oil for deep frying

Garnish:
sliced onion and lemon wedges

Soak split peas overnight, or for at least 6 hours, in water to cover. Drain, grind to a paste in blender or put twice through fine screen of mincer. Mix in the onions, chillies, turmeric and salt. Make small balls and flatten to 12 mm (½ inch) thickness.

Heat oil in a wok and put fritters one at a time into the oil. Fry only 6 or 7 at a time. Spoon hot oil over the fritters until they are golden brown. Drain on absorbent paper. Serve garnished with sliced raw onion and lemon wedges.

VEGETABLE FRITTERS

INDIA

Makes about 30 fritters

In India, a country that is largely vegetarian, one finds vegetables used with a great deal of imagination. These light, crisp morsels are served at tea time but would also be most appropriate as an accompaniment to a meal or as cocktail snacks. If pea flour is not obtainable use ordinary wheat flour. Or lighten both flavour and texture by mixing equal quantities of pea flour and self-raising flour.

1½ cups besan (chick pea flour)
1 teaspoon garam masala (see Glossary)
2 teaspoons salt
½ teaspoon ground turmeric
½ teaspoon chilli powder, optional
1 scant cup water
1 clove garlic, crushed
4 cups mixed chopped potato, onion, eggplant, cauliflower or other raw vegetables
oil for deep frying

Sift into a bowl the flour or mixture of flour with the garam masala, salt, turmeric, chilli powder. Add water gradually, mixing to a thick batter. Stir in garlic and beat well, allow batter to stand for 30 minutes and beat again.

Add vegetables to batter and mix thoroughly. Heat oil to a depth of 10 cm (4 inches) in a wok and test with a drop of batter. When batter rises immediately to the surface, oil is hot enough. Drop teaspoons of mixture into oil and fry over medium heat until fritters are pale golden on both sides. Do not fry too many at once or the temperature of the oil will be lowered too much and the fritters will be greasy and heavy. Lift out with a slotted spoon and drain on absorbent paper.

Just before serving, heat oil again and when almost smoking hot return fritters to wok, a few at a time, for about 30 seconds or until golden brown all over. The second frying makes them very crisp. Drain on paper and serve immediately.

DEVILLED PRAWN CANAPES   SRI LANKA

Makes about 24

A spicy version of a cocktail titbit introduced by the colonials. Serve as a pre-dinner savoury, or at cocktail parties.

6 slices day-old white bread
oil for deep frying
1 large onion, finely chopped
1 clove garlic, finely chopped
½ teaspoon chilli powder
1 teaspoon paprika
2 tablespoons tomato sauce
1 teaspoon salt
500 g (1 lb) small raw prawns,
    shelled and de-veined

With a small circular cutter, cut 4 rounds from each slice of bread. Heat oil in wok and deep fry the bread rounds, a few at a time, until golden brown. Drain on absorbent paper. Pour off oil from wok, leaving about 2 tablespoons.

Add the onions and garlic to the oil and fry on low heat, stirring frequently, until they are soft and golden. Add the chilli powder, paprika, tomato sauce, salt and cook, stirring, until the mixture is a thick paste. Add the prawns and cook, stirring, until they are done. Cool, then top each piece of bread with a prawn.

BEAN SPROUT FRITTERS   BURMA

250 g (8 oz) fresh bean sprouts
1 cup plain four
1 cup lukewarm water
1 tablespoon peanut oil
salt and pepper to taste
1 egg white
oil for deep frying

Dipping Sauce:
1 tablespoon fish sauce
2 tablespoons water
2 teaspoons chilli sauce
¼ teaspoon garlic powder, optional

Wash bean sprouts, drain and dry on kitchen towel. Sift flour into a bowl, add warm water, salt and pepper and beat with a wooden spoon until smooth. Stir in oil and allow to stand for 30 minutes. Just before using, stiffly beat egg white and fold into batter. Mix the bean sprouts through the batter.

Heat oil in wok and deep fry mixture by tablespoons over medium high heat until golden brown. Do not fry too many fritters at a time or temperature of oil will be reduced. Drain on absorbent paper. Serve warm with dipping sauce.

Dipping Sauce: Mix together the ingredients and serve in a small bowl alongside the fritters.

FRIED PRAWN BALLS   BURMA

Serves: 4

500 g (1 lb) raw shelled prawns
2 medium onions
2 fresh green or pickled chillies
3 tablespoons chopped fresh
   coriander leaves
¼ teaspoon ground turmeric
½ teaspoon garlic, crushed
1 teaspoon salt, or to taste
¼ teaspoon ground black pepper
plain flour
oil for frying

De-vein the prawns. Chop very finely the prawns, onions, chillies and coriander leaves and mix well with the turmeric, garlic, salt and black pepper. Shape into 2.5 cm (1 inch) balls and roll in flour to coat.

Heat 2 cups oil in a wok and fry balls for 2 minutes. Drain and serve immediately.

STEAMED MUSHROOMS WITH
PRAWNS   KOREA

Serves: 4-6

250 g (8 oz) fresh mushrooms
250 g (8 oz) peeled raw prawns
6 canned water chestnuts, finely
   chopped
2 tablespoons finely chopped spring
   onion
1 tablespoon cornflour
1 tablespoon light soy sauce
1 teaspoon oyster sauce
½ teaspoon salt
½ teaspoon finely grated fresh ginger
fresh coriander leaves for garnish,
   optional

Choose small mushrooms at the cup stage. Wipe clean with damp paper towels and remove stems, leaving caps intact. De-vein prawns and chop finely. Combine with all other ingredients in a bowl, mixing thoroughly. Fill mushroom caps, mounding filling slightly. Put mushrooms on a heatproof plate which has been lightly oiled, place on steamer rack in wok, cover and steam for 20 minutes. Serve warm or at room temperature, garnished with fresh coriander.

FISH AND SEAFOOD

STIR-FRIED SCALLOPS WITH SNOW PEAS

CHINA

Serves: 2-3

See picture page 38

375 g (12 oz) scallops
2 leeks
125 g (4 oz) snow peas
2 tablespoons peanut oil
1 teaspoon finely grated fresh ginger
2 teaspoons cornflour
¼ cup water
2 teaspoons light soy sauce
salt

Wash and beard scallops and dry well on kitchen paper. Wash leeks thoroughly to get rid of all sand and grit. Slice white part of leeks very fine, diagonally. Remove strings from snow peas.

Heat oil in wok and fry leeks and ginger for 2 minutes over medium heat. Add scallops and fry on high heat, stirring, for 1 minute. Add snow peas and stir fry for just 1 minute longer. Push all these ingredients to side of wok, pour in cornflour mixed with water and soy sauce and stir until thickened, about 1 minute. Stir in scallops and vegetables from side of wok, adjust salt and serve immediately on a bed of braised lettuce.

Note: If leeks are not available, substitute the white part of 10 spring onions cut into 2.5 cm (1 inch) lengths.

DEEP-FRIED HONEYED PRAWNS

CHINA

Serves: 3

See picture page 56

375 g (12 oz) raw, shelled king
    prawns
1 clove garlic
salt and pepper
½ teaspoon sesame oil
1 tablespoon cornflour
3 tablespoons sesame seeds
½ cup self-raising flour
water
oil for deep frying
½ cup honey
steamed broccoli

Wash and de-vein prawns, drain well, then wrap prawns in a clean, dry cloth and firmly press out surplus water. Crush garlic with 1 teaspoon salt, place in a bowl, add pepper, sesame oil and cornflour and mix well. Add prawns, mix and allow to stand while toasting sesame seeds and preparing batter.

Toast the sesame seeds in a dry wok, stirring constantly, over medium heat until the seeds are golden brown. Remove immediately on to a plate to cool. Add sufficient cold water to the self-raising flour to make a coating batter, neither too thick nor too runny.

Heat enough oil for deep frying in a wok, on moderate heat. When oil is ready, a drop of batter should rise immediately to the surface. Dip prawns in batter and add individually to the oil in quick succession. Fry on high heat until they are cooked to a golden colour. Remove prawns with slotted spoon and drain on kitchen paper. Drain oil from wok, wipe over with kitchen paper and heat till warm. Turn off heat and add honey to wok. (The wok should be warm enough to thin the honey slightly.) Add prawns to honey, stir so they are all coated, then transfer to heated serving dish. Sprinkle with toasted sesame seeds, surround with broccoli sprigs and serve immediately with hot white rice.

SZECHWANESE-STYLE SQUID   CHINA

Serves: 4   *See picture page 56*

500 g (1 lb) tender squid
½ teaspoon salt
½ teaspoon monosodium glutamate,
**   optional**
1 tablespoon egg white
1½ tablespoons cornflour
1½ tablespoons peanut oil
1 small red capsicum
1 clove garlic
6 spring onions
½ cup chicken stock or water
½ teaspoon each salt and sugar
1 teaspoon chilli oil
2 teaspoons cornflour
2 tablespoons cold water
peanut oil for deep frying
1 tablespoon preserved radish with
**   chilli**
12 snow peas

Wash squid well. Discard head and inside of squid. Slit body of squid lengthways and cut into 5 cm x 2.5 cm (2 inch x 1 inch) pieces. Rinse well. On inner surface make diagonal slits with a sharp knife, first one way and then the other to give a pattern of small diamonds. Be careful not to cut right through. Combine squid with the first quantity of salt, monosodium glutamate, egg white and cornflour and the 1½ tablespoons peanut oil. Mix thoroughly and set aside while preparing other ingredients.

Remove seeds and membranes from capsicum and cut in thin strips. Chop the garlic finely and cut spring onions in bite-size lengths. Have all ingredients prepared, measured and ready before starting to cook. Combine stock with salt, sugar and chilli oil. In a separate bowl mix the cornflour with the cold water.

Heat 1½ cups peanut oil in wok and when very hot add the squid and fry on high heat for just long enough to cook the squid, about 2 minutes. As it cooks the squid curls, showing the scoring on the inner surface. Do not overcook or it will toughen. Drain contents of wok through wire frying spoon placed over a heatproof bowl.

Return wok to heat with just the oil that clings to the sides. Stir fry snow peas for 1 minute and remove. Add the garlic, red capsicum, radish and spring onions and stir fry over high heat for one minute. Return drained squid to wok.

Add stock mixture and as soon as the liquid comes to the boil stir in the cornflour mixture and stir until it thickens. This should take only a few seconds. Garnish with snow peas and serve immediately with plain white rice.

STEAMED FISH WITH WALNUTS

CHINA

Serves: 4

See picture page 37

1 whole snapper, ocean perch or
    other firm white fish, about 1 kg
    (2 lb)
salt
1 teaspoon finely grated fresh ginger
1 tablespoon light soy sauce
¼ cup peanut oil
¼ cup peeled walnuts
1 tablespoon soy sauce
1 teaspoon sesame oil
3 spring onions, thinly sliced

Clean and scale fish, but leave head and tail on. Dip a piece of dampened kitchen paper in salt and clean out the cavity of the fish carefully. Rinse well. Trim fins and sharp spines with kitchen scissors. Rub fish all over, inside and out, with the ginger and soy sauce. Place on a heatproof dish, put dish on a steaming rack on wok, add 3 cups boiling water, cover the wok and steam the fish for 10-12 minutes, or until fish is cooked. Test at the thickest part and if flesh is milky white and opaque, fish is done.

Lift dish from steamer, cover with foil and keep warm. Dry the wok well, heat oil and fry the walnuts over medium heat just until pale golden. (Peeled walnuts are available at Chinese groceries and are preferable to ordinary walnuts as there is no thin skin to give a bitter taste.)

Lift out walnuts on slotted spoon and drain on absorbent paper. Take 3 tablespoons of the hot oil and pour over the fish. Combine soy sauce and sesame oil and pour over the fish also. Garnish with walnuts and sliced spring onions and serve immediately, accompanied by white rice.

CHILLI-FRIED LOBSTER

SINGAPORE

Serves: 4

2 fresh lobster tails, medium-size
½ cup peanut oil
2 teaspoons finely chopped fresh
    ginger
2 teaspoons finely chopped garlic
1 cup finely chopped spring onions
3 fresh red chillies, seeded and
    chopped
¼ cup tomato sauce
¼ cup chilli sauce
1 tablespoon sugar
2 teaspoons cornflour
2 tablespoons Chinese wine or dry
    sherry
1 tablespoon light soy sauce
2 tablespoons fish sauce
salt

Wash lobster tails and chop into sections. Heat a wok, add oil and when oil is very hot fry the lobster pieces until they change colour, turning them frequently so they cook on all sides. Remote to a plate. Turn heat to low and fry the ginger, garlic, spring onions and red chillies, stirring constantly, until they are soft but not brown. Add the tomato and chilli sauces and sugar. Stir and simmer covered for 2 minutes.

Mix cornflour with Chinese wine, soy and fish sauce and add to the wok. Stir and bring to the boil. Return lobster pieces to the wok, stir to coat with sauce and simmer for 3 minutes on low heat. Add very little water if sauce reduces too much. Adjust salt and serve with hot white rice.

Opposite: Steamed Fish with Walnuts, recipe this page

GARLIC PRAWNS IN COCONUT MILK
PHILIPPINES

Serves: 6

1 kg (2 lb) medium-size raw prawns
1 x 283 ml (10 fl oz) can coconut milk
1 cup water
1 tablespoon finely chopped garlic
1 teaspoon finely chopped fresh ginger
2 teaspoons fish sauce (bagoong balayang)
¼ teaspoon ground black pepper

Shell and de-vein prawns, then wash and dry well on kitchen paper. In a wok, put the coconut milk, water, garlic, ginger, fish sauce and pepper, and bring to the boil, stirring. Reduce heat and simmer uncovered for 10 minutes, stirring frequently. Add prawns and simmer for 10 more minutes, stirring and mixing through the coconut sauce. Serve with hot white rice.

FRIED FISH WITH FIVE SPICE
CHINA

Serves: 4

750 g (1½ lb) fish fillets
1 tablespoon wood fungus
1 cup cornflour
1 teaspoon salt
oil for frying
½ teaspoon five spice powder

Sauce:
1 tablespoon oil
3 spring onions, finely chopped
½ teaspoon finely chopped garlic
1 teaspoon finely chopped ginger
2 tablespoons Chinese wine or dry sherry
2 tablespoons light soy sauce
½ teaspoon five spice powder
2 teaspoons cornflour
2 tablespoons water

Garnish:
½ cup spring onions, sliced thin diagonally

Wash and soak wood fungus in 3 cups of water for 10 minutes, drain and set aside. Cut fish into finger-size pieces, and dust lightly in cornflour, salt and five spice mixture. Heat ½ cup oil in a wok until it just starts to smoke slightly, add half the fish fingers and fry until just cooked, about 3 minutes. Drain on kitchen paper and place on serving dish. Fry the rest of the fish by the same method, place on the serving dish and keep warm.

Clean wok with kitchen paper, heat and add 1 tablespoon oil and stir fry spring onions, garlic and ginger for 2 minutes. Add Chinese wine and soy sauce, lower heat and simmer for 3 minutes. Add five spice powder, stir and add cornflour mixed with water and bring to the boil. Add wood fungus, stir and pour over fish. Garnish with spring onions and serve with hot white rice.

Opposite: Stir-Fried Scallops with Snow Peas, recipe page 33.

FRIED LOBSTER IN BLACK BEAN SAUCE

CHINA

Serves: 4

2 fresh lobster tails, medium-size
1½ tablespoons canned salted black beans
2 cloves garlic, crushed
2 teaspoons sugar
4 tablespoons peanut oil
½ teaspoon garlic, finely chopped
1 teaspoon fresh ginger, finely chopped
¾ cup hot water
2 teaspoons cornflour
2 tablespoons cold water
4 tablespoons chopped spring onions
1 egg, slightly beaten

With a heavy cleaver, chop lobster tails into segments. Rinse black beans in a strainer under cold water for a few seconds, and drain. Mash beans well with crushed garlic and sugar.

Heat oil in a wok and fry garlic and ginger until they start to brown, then add lobster segments, raise heat and stir fry for 4 or 5 minutes, turning them constantly. Remove cooked lobster tail from wok, add black bean mixture to the oil and fry for 1 minute. Add hot water and lobster pieces, stir well, cover and cook for 3 minutes. Stir in cornflour mixed with cold water, stir until sauce boils and thickens, then add spring onions and egg and stir until egg sets. Serve at once with hot white rice.

FRIED FISH WITH CHILLI SAUCE

SINGAPORE

Serves: 4

750 g (1½ lb) white fish fillets
½ teaspoon finely grated fresh ginger
1 teaspoon salt
1 tablespoon cornflour
oil for deep frying

Sauce:
2 tablespoons peanut oil
5 spring onions, chopped
1 teaspoon finely grated fresh ginger
2 teaspoons Chinese chilli sauce
¾ cup chicken or fish stock
185 g (6 oz) crab meat
¼ teaspoon salt
pinch pepper
3 teaspoons cornflour
2 tablespoons cold water

Remove skin from fish, wash and pat dry with paper towels. Lay the fillets on a chopping board and rub with grated ginger. Cut fillets into bite-size pieces and toss in a mixture of salt and cornflour.

Heat peanut oil in a wok and quickly fry the fish, a few pieces at a time, for 1 minute over medium heat. Drain on paper towels and keep warm while preparing sauce. Arrange fish on a dish, spoon sauce over and serve immediately.

Sauce: Heat oil and gently fry spring onions, ginger and chilli sauce for a few seconds, stirring, then add stock, cover and simmer for 3-4 minutes. Add crab meat, heat through for not longer than a minute. Season with salt and pepper. Mix cornflour smoothly with the cold water and stir into sauce. Continue stirring over medium heat until sauce boils and thickens. Taste and adjust seasoning if necessary.

SPICY STEAMED FISH

MALAYSIA

Serves: 4

5 dried Chinese mushrooms
500 g (1 lb) fish fillets
½ teaspoon salt
¼ teaspoon black pepper
sesame oil
3 tablespoons finely shredded
   Chinese preserved vegetables
2 fresh red chillies, finely sliced
2 teaspoons light soy sauce
2 spring onions, finely sliced
3 tablespoons fresh coriander leaves

Soak dried mushrooms in hot water for 30 minutes, then remove stalks and slice caps finely. While mushrooms are soaking wash fish fillets and dry well on paper towels. Season with salt and pepper. Put fish in dish lightly smeared with sesame oil, sprinkle with sliced mushrooms, preserved vegetables and chilli. Sprinkle soy sauce over, cover with foil and steam for 20 minutes. Garnish with spring onions and fresh coriander leaves, and serve with white rice.

FRIED FISH WITH HOT BEAN SAUCE

MALAYSIA

Serves: 4

500 g (1 lb) fish fillets or steaks
2 tablespoons Chinese wine or dry
   sherry
2 teaspoons finely chopped garlic
2 teaspoons finely chopped fresh
   ginger
2 tablespoons hot bean sauce or
   bean sauce with 2 teaspoons chilli
   sauce
plain flour
peanut oil for deep frying
3 tablespoons finely chopped spring
   onions including green portion
1 teaspoon cornflour
2 tablespoons cold water

Garnish:
fresh coriander, chopped (optional)

Score the fish fillets lightly on both sides. Mix together the wine, half the garlic and ginger, and 1 tablespoon of the hot bean sauce. Rub the mixture well into the slashes and all over the fish fillets and allow to marinate for 15 minutes. Drain, reserving marinade. Dry on paper towels and dust with plain flour. Heat 1 cup oil in a wok. Fry one or two pieces of fish at a time until golden brown on both sides. Drain from the oil and put on a warm serving plate.

Pour off all but a tablespoon of oil from the wok. In this fry the remaining garlic and ginger and the chopped spring onions, stirring, until garlic starts to colour. Add hot water to the reserved marinade to make up 1 cup. Stir in the remaining bean sauce. Add this liquid to the pan and bring to the boil, then stir in the cornflour mixed with the cold water and stir constantly until sauce boils and thickens. Pour over the fish and serve immediately with steaming hot white rice. If liked, garnish the fish with chopped fresh coriander.

FRIED PRAWNS WITH SWEET AND SOUR SAUCE

CHINA

Serves: 4

500 g (1 lb) medium-size raw
    prawns
3 cups cold water
salt
½ teaspoon finely grated garlic
½ teaspoon finely grated fresh ginger
1 egg white
3 tablespoons cornflour
peanut oil for deep frying

Garnish:
1 small carrot, sliced
4 spring onion flowers

Sauce:
¼ cup white vinegar
¾ cup pineapple juice
2 tablespoons sugar
½ teaspoon salt
2–3 teaspoons tomato sauce
1 tablespoon arrowroot or cornflour
2 tablespoons cold water

Shell and de-vein the prawns, leaving the tail on. Wash the prawns, then soak them in cold water with half teaspoon salt for 30 minutes. Drain well in a colander and dry on kitchen paper. Put prawns into a dry bowl and sprinkle with another half teaspoon of salt. Add the garlic and ginger and mix well with the hand. Add egg whites and cornflour and mix again until prawns are thoroughly coated. Cover and refrigerate for 4 hours or overnight.

Sauce: Combine vinegar, fruit juice, sugar, salt and tomato sauce. Bring to the boil, remove from heat and stir in arrowroot mixed smoothly with cold water. Return to heat and stir until sauce boils and thickens.

Make the sauce and have it ready at serving time, then heat oil for deep frying (at least 2 cups of oil in a wok). When oil is hot add half the prawns and fry for 1 minute or less — just until prawns turn opaque and pink. Do not overcook or they will lose their succulence and become tough. Lift out on wire spoon and drain on kitchen paper. Let oil get hot again and fry remaining prawns. After draining, put all the prawns on serving dish and pour sauce over. Garnish with sliced carrot and spring onion flowers and serve at once.

Note: To use carrot for garnish, cut V-shaped wedges along length of carrot, then cut in thin slices across. To make spring onion flowers, cut 10 cm (4 inch) lengths of spring onion, using green leaves as well as white portion. With a sharp knife cut one end into fine strips. Soak in iced water and the strips will curl outwards.

STIR-FRIED HONEY PRAWNS

CHINA

Serves: 4

500 g (1 lb) raw prawns
2 tablespoons peanut oil
1 red capsicum, diced
1 green capsicum, diced
½ teaspoon finely chopped fresh
  ginger
½ cup strong chicken stock
1 tablespoon honey
1 tablespoon Chinese wine or dry
  sherry
1 tablespoon light soy sauce
1 teaspoon cornflour
2 tablespoons cold water

Shell and de-vein prawns, leaving the tails on. Heat wok, add oil and stir fry red and green capsicums for 1 minute and push to the side of wok. Add chopped ginger and prawns and stir fry on medium heat until colour changes then push up the sides of wok. Add stock, honey, Chinese wine and soy sauce. Now add cornflour mixed with cold water to wok and stir mixture till it thickens. Bring all ingredients from sides of wok, stir and serve at once accompanied by white rice.

ABALONE AND MUSHROOMS WITH OYSTER SAUCE

SINGAPORE

Serves: 4

1 x 454 g (1 lb) can abalone
6 dried Chinese mushrooms
3 Chinese mustard cabbage leaves
4 spring onions

Sauce:
1½ tablespoons oyster sauce
2 teaspoons light soy sauce
1 tablespoon Chinese wine or dry
  sherry
3 teaspoons cornflour
1 cup liquid from can of abalone

Drain liquid from can of abalone and reserve. Slice abalone in paper-thin slices. Soak mushrooms in hot water for 30 minutes, then cut off and discard stalks and slice each mushroom into 4. Cut cabbage into bite-size pieces and spring onions into similar lengths.

Sauce: Combine oyster sauce, soy sauce and wine, add a little to the cornflour and mix until smooth, then combine with abalone liquid made up to 1 cup with water if necessary. Bring to the boil in a wok, stirring constantly. Add mushrooms, cabbage and spring onions. Cook, stirring until the vegetables are tender but still crisp, about 2 minutes. Add abalone and just heat through. Do not cook abalone on high heat or for longer than is necessary to just heat it or it will toughen.

STEAMED SESAME FISH PARCELS

BURMA

Serves: 4

750 g (1½ lb) fish fillets
8 large lettuce or spinach leaves for
    wrapping
¾ cup desiccated coconut
½ cup hot water
2 teaspoons finely chopped garlic
1 tablespoon finely chopped fresh
    ginger
3 tablespoons toasted sesame seeds
1 teaspoon salt
1 teaspoon ground turmeric
½ teaspoon ground black pepper
½ teaspoon chilli powder
juice of half a lemon
2 tablespoons rice flour
3 tablespoons chopped fresh
    coriander leaves

Wash and dry fillets. Place lettuce or spinach leaves in container, pour boiling water over and set aside to soften. Put coconut, hot water, garlic and ginger in blender container, blend until coconut is very finely ground. Turn into a bowl, mix in other ingredients. Divide fish fillets into eight portions, place each on a lettuce or spinach leaf, top with 1 tablespoon of coconut mixture, wrap and arrange on a heat-proof plate. Place plate on a rack above boiling water in a wok, cover with lid and steam for 15 minutes. Serve hot with rice.

CHILLI PRAWNS WITH BRAISED BAMBOO SHOOTS

SINGAPORE

Serves: 6

500 g (1 lb) raw prawns
1 cup cold water
½ teaspoon salt
3 teaspoons cornflour
1 tablespoon peanut oil
½ egg white, beaten slightly
½ teaspoon salt

Seasonings and Sauce:
8 large dried chillies
1 teaspoon cornflour
2 teaspoons cold water
1 tablespoon light soy sauce
1 tablespoon Chinese wine or dry
** sherry**
2 teaspoons honey or sugar
1 teaspoon white vinegar
½ teaspoon salt
½ teaspoon black pepper
3 tablespoons peanut oil
4 spring onions, finely chopped
1 teaspoon finely chopped fresh
** ginger**
2 teaspoons finely chopped garlic
1 x 397 g (14 oz) can braised bamboo
** shoots**

Shell and de-vein prawns, put in a bowl and add cold water and salt. Stir and leave for 2 minutes, then rinse under cold tap for 1 minute, and drain well. Sprinkle prawns with cornflour and peanut oil and mix well. Leave for 15 minutes, add egg white and salt. Mix well, leave for 30 minutes.

Prepare seasonings and sauce. Break or cut tops off chillies, shake out and discard seeds. Mix cornflour and water in small bowl, then stir in light soy, wine, honey, vinegar, salt and pepper. Set aside.

Heat wok, add the oil and when hot, fry the chillies over medium heat until they are almost black. This takes only a few seconds, and they should be stirred all the while. Remove chillies from wok and drain on kitchen paper. Drain any excess marinade from prawns, add prawns to wok and stir fry over high heat. The prawns must not be overcooked. Fifteen seconds is enough for small, 35 seconds for large prawns. Add spring onions, bamboo shoots, ginger and garlic and stir fry briefly. Stir seasonings mixture again to blend the cornflour smoothly, add to the wok, stirring constantly until cornflour boils and thickens. Turn off heat. Return chillies to the wok, stir to mix and serve immediately with white rice.

FRIED FISH WITH MUSHROOMS

THAILAND

Serves: 4

750 g (1½ lb) fish fillets
6 dried Chinese mushrooms
3 tablespoons peanut oil
6 spring onions, cut into 2.5 cm
(1 inch) pieces
3 teaspoons finely chopped garlic
3 teaspoons finely chopped fresh
ginger
1 tablespoon light soy sauce
1½ tablespoons brown sugar
1 tablespoon lemon juice
1 tablespoon fish sauce
¼ teaspoon ground black pepper
2 tablespoons chopped fresh
coriander leaves
2 fresh red chillies, sliced

Soak dried mushrooms in hot water for 30 minutes, then remove stalks and slice caps finely. While mushrooms are soaking, wash fish fillets and dry well on paper towels. Heat oil in wok and fry half the fillets on both sides until cooked, about 2 minutes. Remove fish to serving platter and keep warm. Fry the rest of the fish, remove and keep warm.

Let oil cool slightly, then fry the spring onions until soft, add garlic, ginger and mushrooms and cook on low heat, stirring until soft and golden. Add soy sauce, brown sugar, lemon juice, fish sauce and pepper and simmer for 1 minute. Pour over the fish, garnish with coriander leaves and chillies and serve at once with white rice.

BURRIDA

ITALIAN FISH STEW

Serves: 4

750 g (1½ lb) fish fillets
2 tablespoons olive oil
2 medium onions, finely chopped
1 teaspoon finely chopped garlic
2 anchovy fillets, finely chopped
1 teaspoon dried oregano
1 tablespoon finely chopped parsley
3 large tomatoes, peeled and chopped
1 cup dry white wine
¼ teaspoon ground black pepper
salt to taste

Heat wok, add oil and when hot add onions, garlic and finely chopped anchovy fillets. Stir fry on medium heat till onions are soft and lightly browned. Add oregano, parsley and peeled tomatoes and continue stirring till tomatoes are cooked to a pulp. Add wine and black pepper, stir and simmer gently for 1 minute. Place the fish fillets in the wok, spoon tomato mixture over fish, cover and simmer for 15 minutes. Adjust seasoning, and serve hot with crusty bread.

FRIED FISH WITH HOT SAUCE   INDONESIA

Serves: 4-6

1 kg (2 lb) fish steaks
peanut oil for frying
1 large onion, finely chopped
1 teaspoon finely chopped garlic
2 teaspoons finely chopped fresh
   ginger
1 teaspoon dried shrimp paste (trasi)
3 teaspoons sambal ulek or chilli
   sauce
2 teaspoons finely grated lemon rind
1 teaspoon laos powder
2 tablespoons lemon juice
2 tablespoons palm sugar or
   substitute
2 tablespoons dark soy sauce
salt

Wash fish steaks and dry on kitchen paper. If large, cut into serving portions. Heat 1 cup oil in a wok and when hot fry half the fish steaks until golden brown, on both sides. Drain, put on serving dish and keep warm. Follow this method with the remaining fish steaks.

Pour off all but 2 tablespoons oil from wok and fry the onion until soft, on low heat. Add garlic, ginger and trasi, and stir over medium heat until golden brown. Add sambal ulek, lemon rind, laos, lemon juice, sugar and soy sauce. Stir and simmer for 2 or 3 more minutes. Adjust salt and spoon sauce over fish fillets. Serve immediately with hot white rice.

FRIED FISH WITH VEGETABLES   CAMBODIA

Serves: 4-6

750 g (1½ lb) white fish fillets
250 g (8 oz) cellophane noodles
1 tablespoon egg white
½ teaspoon salt
1 cup cornflour
6 tablespoons oil
2 teaspoons finely chopped garlic
1 teaspoon finely chopped fresh
   ginger
2 cups sliced white Chinese cabbage
6 spring onions, cut in 2.5 cm
   (1 inch) lengths
2 tablespoons fish sauce
1 teaspoon extra cornflour
¼ cup cold water

Wash fish, dry well on kitchen paper and cut into finger pieces. Soak noodles in hot water 15 minutes, then drop into lightly salted boiling water and cook 5 minutes. Drain and cut into short lengths and set aside.

Dip fish fingers in egg white and then in a mixture of salt and cornflour. Dust off excess flour. Heat oil in a wok and fry fish on high heat (one-third of the quantity of fish at a time) for just long enough to cook it through. This should take from 1-2 minutes depending on the thickness of the fish. Drain on kitchen paper and keep warm.

Pour off all but 2 tablespoons of the oil, add garlic, ginger, cabbage and stir fry for 1 minute. Add spring onions and fish sauce and stir fry for 1 minute more. Add extra cornflour mixed with the cold water. Stir until the sauce boils and thickens. Arrange cellophane noodles on a serving dish and spread with the cooked vegetables. Place fish pieces on top and serve immediately.

POULTRY

STIR-FRIED CHICKEN WITH CAPSICUMS

CHINA

Serves: 4

500 g (1 lb) chicken breasts
4 dried Chinese mushrooms
1 tablespoons Chinese wine or dry
  sherry
2 tablespoons light soy sauce
1 teaspoon finely chopped fresh
  ginger
1 teaspoon finely chopped garlic
½ teaspoon salt
¼ teaspoon pepper, optional
2 tablespoons peanut oil
1 small red capsicum, cut in thin
  strips
1 small green capsicum, cut in thin
  strips
½ cup chicken stock
2 teaspoons cornflour
1 tablespoon cold water

Garnish:
2 tablespoons sweet sliced cucumbers
  (bottled)
4 spring onion flowers

Bone and skin chicken breasts, put bones and skin into a small saucepan with water to cover and simmer to make stock. Cut chicken meat into bite-size pieces and marinate in the wine, 1 tablespoon soy sauce, half the ginger and garlic, salt and pepper. Soak the mushrooms in hot water for 30 minutes. Squeeze out excess water, discard stems, slice the caps and set aside.

Heat the wok, add oil and swirl to coat the inside of the wok, then add chicken and stir fry for 1 minute on high heat. Remove to a plate. Lower heat, add remaining ginger and garlic, sliced mushrooms and the capsicums and stir fry for 2 minutes. Add remaining soy mixed with chicken stock. Mix cornflour smoothly with the cold water and stir into liquid in wok until it boils and thickens. Return chicken and heat through. Transfer to serving dish and garnish with sweet sliced cucumber and spring onion flowers. Serve with hot white rice.

Note: To make spring onion flowers, cut 10 cm (4 inch) lengths of the green portion of spring onions, fringe ends with a sharp pointed knife and refrigerate in a bowl of water until ends curl. Prepare these before starting to cook the chicken.

CHICKEN STEW   AUSTRALIA

Serves: 4-6

See picture page 55

1.25 kg (2½ lb) roasting chicken
  or chicken pieces
1 bay leaf
¼ cup celery tops
salt and pepper
2 tablespoons butter
1 tablespoon oil
1 large onion, diced
½ teaspoon finely chopped garlic
1 cup diced turnip or parsnip
2 cups diced carrots
2 cups sliced celery stalks
2 cups chicken stock
½ cup tomato puree
¼ teaspoon dried tarragon
¼ teaspoon dried thyme
2 large potatoes, peeled and sliced
  thick
1 small bunch broccoli, cut into
  sprigs
1 tablespoon plain flour

Joint chicken, cut off wing tips and place these together with the neck and back pieces in a saucepan with 5 cups of water, 1 teaspoon salt, bay leaf and celery tops and simmer to make stock, about 30 minutes.

Heat wok, add oil and half the butter and stir fry the garlic and all the vegetables over high heat for 2-3 minutes. Cover and cook for 2 more minutes. Add chicken pieces, stock, tomato purée, 1 teaspoon salt, ¼ teaspoon pepper, tarragon and thyme. Bring to the boil, then reduce heat, cover and simmer for 15-20 minutes or until chicken is almost tender. Add potatoes and cook covered for another 10 minutes. Finally add the broccoli sprigs, making sure they sit on top of the stew and cook in the steam for the next 10 minutes. The bright green of the cooked broccoli also serves as a garnish for the dish.

In a bowl, mix flour with the remaining tablespoon of butter and add, a little at a time, to the gravy, stirring to make sure it is well blended. Allow to boil and thicken. Serve hot, accompanied by crusty bread.

SAUTÉED CHICKEN BREASTS WITH MUSHROOMS AND TARRAGON

FRANCE

Serves: 4

2 large chicken breasts (approx. 750 g or 1½ lb)
½ teaspoon salt
¼ teaspoon pepper
2 tablespoons cornflour
2 tablespoons olive oil
60 g (2 oz) clarified butter (ghee) or unsalted butter
250 g (8 oz) button mushrooms, sliced
1 cup chicken stock
½ cup dry white wine
1 teaspoon dried tarragon
1 tablespoon cold water
½ cup fresh cream
salt to taste

Stock:
2 cups water
1 small onion
celery leaves
peppercorns
salt

Skin and bone chicken breasts. Make required stock by boiling the skin and bones with 2 cups water, 1 small onion, few celery leaves, few peppercorns and ¼ teaspoon salt until reduced to 1 cup.

Cut meat from each chicken breast into 4 pieces. Season the pieces well with salt and pepper and set aside for 15 minutes. Sprinkle with half the cornflour and then with half the olive oil, mix well and leave for a further 15 minutes.

Heat butter and remaining oil in wok, and over medium heat, fry the chicken pieces for 2 minutes, turning them to cook on all sides. Push chicken up the side of wok and add the sliced mushrooms. Cook, stirring for 2 minutes. Add stock, wine and tarragon, return chicken, stir through, cover and simmer on low heat for about 8 minutes. Thicken with remaining cornflour mixed with cold water.

Add cream and heat through without boiling. Adjust seasoning and serve immediately with buttered rice or crusty bread.

CHICKEN PAPRIKA   HUNGARY

Serves: 4

2 large chicken breasts approx. 750 g
  (1½ lb)
2 tablespoons plain flour
1 teaspoon salt
3 teaspoons paprika
2 tablespoons oil
1 tablespoon butter
1 large onion, finely chopped
1 teaspoon finely chopped garlic
1 tablespoon finely chopped parsley
1 cup chicken stock
1 tablespoon tomato paste
½ cup sour cream
salt and white pepper to taste

Chop each breast into six equal pieces. Season flour with salt and 1 teaspoon of the paprika and coat chicken pieces. Heat wok, add oil and when hot stir fry the chicken in two lots until golden. Remove chicken to a plate when all the pieces have been fried. Add butter and fry onions and garlic on low heat, stirring, until soft and golden. Add parsley and remaining paprika, chicken stock and tomato paste. Stir briefly and return chicken to the wok.

Cover and simmer until chicken is tender, about 15 minutes. Just before serving, stir in the sour cream and heat through without letting it boil. Taste and adjust seasoning and serve with hot buttered noodles.

BRAISED SESAME CHICKEN
AND MUSHROOMS   KOREA

Serves: 4-6

8 dried Chinese mushrooms
1 kg (2 lb) chicken breasts or thighs
3 tablespoons light soy sauce
1 tablespoon sesame oil
1 teaspoon finely chopped garlic
1 teaspoon cayenne pepper or chilli
  powder
½ teaspoon ground black pepper
2 tablespoons oil
1 medium onion
2 canned bamboo shoots
4 spring onions
3 tablespoons toasted, crushed sesame
  seeds

Soak mushrooms in hot water for 30 minutes, drain and reserve liquid. Discard stems and slice caps into thin strips. With a heavy cleaver, chop chicken into serving pieces, rinse in cold water to remove any bone fragments and dry on kitchen paper. Combine soy sauce, sesame oil, garlic, cayenne pepper and black pepper, rub well over chicken pieces and marinate in this mixture for 30 minutes.

Heat oil in a wok and stir fry the well-drained pieces over high heat until brown. Add mushroom strips, half cup of mushroom liquid and the remaining marinade from chicken. Cover and simmer for 15 minutes. Meanwhile, cut onion into 4 wedges, divide each wedge in halves crossways and separate layers of onion. Cut bamboo shoots into quarters, then into slices. Cut spring onions into bite-size lengths, using both green and white portions. Add to simmering chicken and cook for a further 3 minutes. Sprinkle with crushed sesame seeds and serve with hot white rice.

BRAISED CHICKEN WITH VEGETABLES

CHINA

Serves: 4-6

750 g (1½ lb) chicken thighs or
    breasts
1 teaspoon five spice powder
6 dried Chinese mushrooms
2 cups boiling water
1 tablespoon wood fungus, optional
1 red capsicum
6 spring onions
2 tablespoons peanut oil
1 teaspoon finely chopped garlic
1 teaspoon finely chopped fresh
    ginger
2 tablespoons light soy sauce
2 tablespoons Chinese wine or dry
    sherry
1 canned bamboo shoot
1 tablespoon oyster sauce
1½ cups mushroom liquid
1 tablespoon cornflour

Garnish:
spring onion curls

Use a heavy cleaver and chop chicken into serving portions. Rinse in cold water, carefully removing any bone fragments. Dry the chicken on kitchen paper, sprinkle over with five spice powder and set aside.

Pour 2 cups boiling water over mushrooms, soak for 30 minutes. Squeeze out excess water, remove and discard stalks, slice caps. Reserve soaking liquid. Soak wood fungus in cold water 15 minutes, drain, cut into bite-size pieces, discarding any tough and gritty portions. Thinly slice the capsicum. Cut one spring onion into 10 cm (4 inch) lengths, fringe both ends with a sharp knife and soak in iced water to curl, set aside for garnish. Cut remaining spring onions into bite-size lengths, about 5 cm (2 inches).

Heat a wok, add peanut oil and swirl, fry the chicken pieces in two lots over high heat until golden. Remove to a plate. Lower heat, add garlic and ginger and fry, stirring, until pale golden. Add soy sauce, wine or sherry, mushrooms and 1 cup of the mushroom liquid. Return chicken to the wok, bring to the boil, cover and simmer on low heat for 15 minutes. Add bamboo shoot, capsicum, spring onions and oyster sauce. Stir well and simmer 5 minutes longer.

Mix cornflour smoothly with remaining ½ cup mushroom liquid and stir into gravy until it boils and thickens. Add wood fungus, stir through, serve hot garnished with the spring onion curls and accompanied by white rice.

STIR-FRIED MARINATED CHICKEN

JAPAN

Serves: 4

2 tablespoons sesame seeds
500 g (1 lb) boned chicken meat
2 tablespoons Japanese soy sauce
2 tablespoons sake or dry sherry
2 teaspoons sugar
4 tablespoons cornflour
1 tablespoon peanut oil
1 tablespoon sesame oil
4 crisp lettuce leaves

In a dry wok, toast sesame seeds over medium low heat, stirring constantly, until they are evenly golden. Turn on to a plate to cool.

Cut chicken meat into bite-size pieces and marinate in a mixture of soy, sake and sugar for 1 hour. Drain chicken well, roll pieces in cornflour and set aside for 10 minutes.

Heat both oils in a wok, and stir fry chicken on medium high heat for about 2-3 minutes or until golden brown and crisp. Drain on kitchen paper, place on lettuce leaves and serve hot sprinkled with toasted sesame seeds.

BRAISED CHICKEN WITH FRESH MUSHROOMS

BURMA

Serves: 4

500 g (1 lb) fresh mushrooms
500 g (1 lb) chicken thighs or
    breasts
3 tablespoons peanut oil
1 large onion, finely sliced
1 teaspoon turmeric
3 teaspoons finely chopped garlic
1 peeled tomato, chopped
1 tablespoon light soy sauce
½ cup hot stock or water
2 tablespoons fish sauce
2 teaspoons chilli sauce
½ teaspoon sesame oil
salt to taste

Wipe mushrooms with damp kitchen paper. Do not wash. If large, cut in quarters. Chop chicken pieces with cleaver into serving-size portions, rinse to remove any chips of bone, and wipe on kitchen paper.

Heat wok, add oil and when hot fry onion, turmeric and garlic until golden brown. Add chicken pieces and stir fry for 2 minutes, on high heat, then cover and simmer for 3 minutes on medium heat. Add chopped tomato, soy sauce, stock, fish sauce, chilli sauce and mushrooms. Stir, cover and simmer for 20 minutes. Add sesame oil, raise heat and cook uncovered until most of the liquid has evaporated. Adjust seasoning and serve hot with rice.

STEAMED CHICKEN AND MUSHROOMS WITH FISH SAUCE

VIETNAM

Serves: 4-6

1 kg (2 lb) chicken breasts
6 dried Chinese mushrooms
1 tablespoon finely shredded ginger
4 spring onions, sliced diagonally
¾ teaspoon ground black pepper
2 tablespoons fish sauce
1 tablespoon light soy sauce
1 teaspoon finely chopped garlic
1 teaspoon salt
2 teaspoons sesame oil
2 cups, soaked and drained, cellophane noodles
4 tablespoons chopped fresh coriander

Garnish:
fresh coriander, chopped

Pour hot water over cellophane noodles in a bowl, let stand for 15 minutes, then drain. Pour hot water over Chinese mushrooms and soak for 30 minutes. Squeeze out excess water, cut off and discard mushroom stems and cut the caps into thick slices. Chop chicken breasts into bite-size pieces, place in a bowl and add mushrooms, ginger, spring onions, black pepper, fish sauce, soy, garlic, salt and sesame oil and mix well.

Chop the cellophane noodles into bite-size lengths and place in a heatproof dish. Sprinkle half the coriander over the noodles then spread the chicken mixture. Place dish on a rack over boiling water in a wok, cover and steam for 35 minutes, adding more boiling water as necessary. Garnish with remaining coriander and serve hot.

Opposite: Chicken Stew, recipe page 49.

STIR-FRIED CHICKEN WITH OYSTER SAUCE

CHINA

Serves: 4

500 g (1 lb) chicken breasts
¼ teaspoon crushed garlic
½ teaspoon grated fresh ginger
½ teaspoon salt
6 large dried Chinese mushrooms
2 celery stalks
3 spring onions
2 tablespoons peanut oil
1 tablespoon light soy sauce
½ cup mushroom liquid
2 tablespoons Chinese wine or dry sherry

2 teaspoons cornflour
1 tablespoon cold water
1 tablespoon oyster sauce

Remove skin then bone the chicken breasts and cut the meat into dice. Mix with garlic, ginger and salt and set aside. Soak mushrooms in bowl of hot water for 30 minutes, squeeze out excess water and cut into slices. Reserve liquid. Cut celery diagonally into thin slices and cut the spring onions into short lengths.

Heat 1 tablespoon oil in a wok and stir fry the vegetables for 2 minutes. Push them up the side of wok. Add 1 tablespoon oil, raise heat, add chicken and stir fry until chicken changes colour. Add soy sauce, mushroom liquid, and sherry and bring to the boil. Mix cornflour with cold water and oyster sauce and stir into liquid, bring to boil and stir until thick. Serve immediately with hot white rice.

CHICKEN CURRY WITH COCONUT MILK

MALAYSIA

Serves: 6

1 x 1 kg (2 lb) chicken
1 bamboo shoot, canned
3 tablespoons peanut oil
2 medium onions, chopped
1 teaspoon finely chopped garlic
2 tablespoons ground coriander
1 teaspoon dried shrimp paste (blacan)
1 teaspoon laos powder
4 strips lemon rind, chopped
1 teaspoon chilli powder
1 teaspoon salt
1 cup water
1 cup thick coconut milk

Joint chicken. Drain bamboo shoot and cut into quarters lengthways, then into slices. Heat wok, add oil and when hot fry onions and garlic over medium heat, stirring, until soft and golden. Add coriander, blacan, laos, lemon rind, chilli powder and salt and fry, stirring constantly, for a few minutes until spices are brown and smell cooked. Add chicken pieces, raise heat, and stir fry until pieces are well coated with the spices, about 5 minutes. Add water, bring to the boil and simmer covered, on low heat, for 20 minutes. Add bamboo shoot, stir and simmer for a further 15 minutes or until chicken is tender. Add thick coconut milk, stir and simmer uncovered, until oil rises to the surface. Serve with hot boiled rice.

Note: If using canned coconut milk or creamed coconut, dilute according to instructions.

Opposite: Szechwanese-Style Squid, recipe page 35, and Deep-Fried Honeyed Prawns, recipe page 34.

CHICKEN WITH CASHEWS

CHINA

Serves: 6

1 x 1.5 kg (3 lb) roasting chicken
1½ teaspoons salt
½ teaspoon five spice powder
250 g (8 oz) snow peas or 1½ cups
    sliced celery
approx. ¼ cup cornflour
1 cup peanut oil
1 cup raw cashews
1 teaspoon crushed garlic
1 teaspoon finely grated fresh ginger
½ cup chicken stock
1 tablespoon light soy sauce
1 teaspoon sugar, optional
2 teaspoons cornflour mixed with 1
    tablespoon cold water

The wok is used to good effect in this recipe — first for steaming, then for deep frying and finally for stir-frying and finishing the dish.

Cut the chicken into serving pieces. Remove wing tips and use these and the back pieces for stock. Rub the chicken pieces with salt and five spice powder, put them in a heatproof dish and place on a rack in wok. Pour water into wok to come below level of rack, cover and steam chicken for 35-45 minutes. Reserve any liquid that collects in dish for adding with stock at end of cooking. While chicken steams, string snow peas or cut celery in diagonal slices.

Coat the chicken pieces with cornflour. Pour off water from wok, heat wok until it is quite dry and add the cup of oil. Heat, then fry the cashews on medium low heat, stirring, until they are golden brown. Remove on slotted spoon and drain on absorbent paper. Fry the chicken pieces, a few at a time, until golden brown on all sides. As each batch is browned, remove to a plate and keep warm.

Pour all but 1 tablespoon of oil from wok and on low heat fry the garlic and ginger, stirring constantly. Add snow peas or finely sliced celery and stir fry for 2 minutes or until colour brightens and vegetables are tender but still crisp. Add chicken stock, including liquid from steaming, soy sauce, sugar. Bring quickly to the boil, stir in cornflour mixed with water and stir for the few seconds needed for sauce to thicken and become clear. Return chicken and cashews to wok, stir just to combine, and serve immediately with rice.

HONEY BRAISED CHICKEN
WITH TOASTED SESAME   CHINA

Serves: 4-6

750 g (1½ lb) chicken thighs
250 g (½ lb) belly pork, diced
2 tablespoons peanut oil
½ cup dark soy sauce
3 tablespoons honey
½ teaspoon five spice powder
3 tablespoons Chinese wine or dry
   sherry
½ teaspoon finely chopped garlic
1 teaspoon finely chopped fresh
   ginger
3 tablespoons toasted sesame seeds

Garnish:
spring onion flowers

Chop each chicken thigh into two pieces. Dice pork. Heat wok, add oil and stir fry the diced pork on high heat for 2 minutes. Add the chicken pieces and stir fry until browned. Add soy, honey, five spice, wine, garlic and ginger and stir well. Reduce heat to low, cover and simmer about 30 minutes or until chicken and pork are tender. Towards end of cooking, stir frequently to make sure the honey glaze does not burn. Sprinkle with sesame seeds and garnish with spring onion flowers. Serve warm with hot white rice.

Note: This recipe can use a whole chicken, cut up, instead of only the thighs.

STIR-FRIED GINGER CHICKEN
WITH BAMBOO SHOOT   THAILAND

Serves: 4

2 large chicken breasts
½ cup dried wood fungus
4 tablespoons finely shredded fresh
   ginger
1 canned bamboo shoot, shredded
1 medium onion, thinly sliced
2 tablespoons lard or peanut oil
2 teaspoons garlic, finely chopped
1 tablespoon light soy sauce
2 tablespoons fish sauce
1 tablespoon vinegar
2 teaspoons sugar
5 spring onions, finely chopped
4 tablespoons fresh coriander leaves,
   chopped

Remove skin and bones from chicken breasts and cut the meat into dice. Soak wood fungus in hot water for 15 minutes, wash well to remove any grit and cut into bite-size pieces. To shred ginger, thinly peel off outer skin, cut into very thin slices, then cut slices into long thread-like strips. Soak ginger in lightly salted water for 10 minutes, then squeeze out moisture. This makes the ginger less pungent.

Heat wok, add lard or oil and on medium low heat fry the onion until soft. Add garlic and stir until garlic starts to turn golden. Add the chicken meat, ginger and bamboo shoot and stir fry for 2 minutes, on medium high heat. Now add the sauces, vinegar and sugar, and when liquid boils reduce heat, cover and simmer 3 minutes. Stir in wood fungus, spring onions and coriander leaves and serve with hot white rice.

BRAISED CHICKEN WITH PLUM SAUCE

CHINA

Serves: 4-6

1 kg (2 lb) chicken thighs and
   breasts
2 tablespoons oil
1 teaspoon finely chopped garlic
1 teaspoon finely chopped fresh
   ginger
2 tablespoons Chinese wine or dry
   sherry
2 tablespoons plum sauce (see
   Glossary)
1 tablespoon light soy sauce
2 teaspoons cornflour
3 tablespoons cold water
4 spring onions cut into 4 cm (1½
   inch) lengths

Garnish:
2 tablespoons finely shredded red
   ginger (see Glossary)

Chop chicken into bite-size pieces. Heat a wok, add oil and swirl to coat inside of wok. Add chicken pieces and stir fry on high heat till brown. Lower heat, add garlic, ginger and stir 1 minute then add Chinese wine, plum sauce and light soy. Stir with chicken, cover and simmer for 30 minutes, stirring every 10 minutes. Mix cornflour and cold water and add to wok, raise heat to medium and stir till sauce thickens. Add spring onions and stir to mix through chicken, for 1 minute. Serve garnished with shredded red ginger.

BRAISED CHICKEN AND MUSHROOMS WITH FISH SAUCE

CAMBODIA

Serves: 4-6

8 dried Chinese mushrooms
1 kg (2 lb) chicken breasts and
  thighs
2 tablespoons lard or oil
3 teaspoons finely chopped garlic
1 teaspoon finely chopped fresh
  ginger
4 tablespoons finely chopped spring
  onions
1 cup reserved mushroom liquid
2 tablespoons fish sauce
1 teaspoon sugar
1 tablespoon cornflour
2 tablespoons cold water

Garnish:
3 tablespoons chopped coriander
  leaves

Soak mushrooms for 30 minutes in hot water. Squeeze dry and reserve soaking liquid. Cut off and discard stems and cut caps into thick slices. Chop chicken into bite-size pieces. Heat wok, add lard and fry garlic and ginger for a few seconds. Add chicken pieces, raise heat and stir fry until chicken loses its pinkness.

Move chicken to side of wok, add spring onions, lower heat and stir fry for 2 minutes until soft. Add mushroom liquid, mushrooms, fish sauce and sugar and mix with chicken pieces. Cover wok and braise for 15 minutes on low heat. Thicken sauce in wok with cornflour mixed with cold water. Garnish with chopped coriander and serve with hot white rice.

CHICKEN AND PORK WITH PEANUT SAUCE

PHILIPPINES

Serves: 6-8

1 x 1.5 kg (3 lb) roasting chicken
500 g (1 lb) pork
125 g (4 oz) raw ham
salt and pepper to taste

Sauce:
½ cup uncooked rice
4 tablespoons lard
1 teaspoon annatto seeds (see Glossary)
1 teaspoon crushed garlic
2 onions, finely chopped
2 tablespoons pork fat, diced
½ cup ground peanuts or peanut butter

Remove skin and bones from chicken. Cut chicken meat into large squares. Cut fat from pork, dice finely and reserve 2 tablespoons for use in the sauce. Cut pork into pieces the same size as chicken. Dice the ham. Put meats into wok with water to barely cover. Add salt and pepper to taste. Bring to a simmer, cover and simmer gently until meat is tender. Turn into a dish and wash out wok.

Sauce: Dry wok over heat. Put uncooked rice into wok and roast over low heat, stirring constantly, until golden. Pound with mortar and pestle or grind to a powder in electric blender. Heat lard in wok and fry annatto seeds over low heat for about 1 minute, by which time oil should have taken on a bright orange colour. Cover pan as seeds tend to spatter and jump. Lift out seeds with draining spoon and discard. In the coloured oil fry the garlic, onions and pork fat until soft and golden brown.

Mix the ground rice with enough stock (from cooking chicken and pork) to make a smooth cream. Add to wok with ground peanuts or peanut butter. Cook until sauce boils, adding more liquid as necessary to give the sauce a good pouring consistency. Heat meats through in the sauce and serve with hot rice.

CHICKEN AND ALMONDS WITH STRAW MUSHROOMS
CHINA

Serves: 4-6

2 whole chicken breasts, boned
½ teaspoon five spice powder
1 tablespoon Chinese wine or dry
  sherry
1 tablespoon light soy sauce
½ teaspoon salt
1 teaspoon sesame oil
1 tablespoon cornflour
2 tablespoons cold water
1 cup chicken stock
2 tablespoons oyster sauce
oil for frying
¾ cup blanched almonds
60 g (2 oz) canned bamboo shoot,
  sliced
¾ cup canned straw mushrooms
4 spring onions sliced into 2.5 cm (1
  inch) lengths

Cut chicken breasts into bite-size pieces and add to a bowl with five spice powder, wine, soy sauce, salt and sesame oil and marinate 10 minutes. Mix cornflour with cold water. Mix stock and oyster sauce and set aside.

Heat wok, add 1 cup oil and fry almonds until golden, drain and set aside. Pour off all but 2 tablespoons oil. Add chicken pieces and stir fry for 1 minute on high heat till chicken changes colour. Add sliced bamboo shoot and straw mushrooms, stir together with chicken for 2 minutes, then move to sides of wok. Add stock and bring to boil.

Add cornflour mixture and stir till sauce thickens, add spring onions then mix and stir all ingredients together. Garnish with fried almonds and serve immediately with hot white rice or noodles.

BRAISED DUCK WITH SALTED YELLOW BEANS

CHINA

Serves: 6

1 x 2 kg (4 lb) duck
1 tablespoon dark soy sauce
3 tablespoons Chinese wine or dry
  sherry
1 teaspoon sugar
3 tablespoons oil
1 teaspoon finely grated or crushed
  garlic
1 teaspoon finely grated fresh
  ginger
3 tablespoons salted yellow beans,
  mashed
4 spring onions cut into 2.5 cm (1
  inch) lengths
4 cups stock or hot water
2 teaspoons cornflour
3 tablespoons cold water

Garnish:
1 cup fresh coriander sprigs
¼ cup red capsicum, shredded
¼ cup green capsicum, shredded

Place duck in boiling water for ½ minute, remove and leave to cool. Mix soy, wine and sugar and rub over duck, both inside and out, and leave to marinate 30 minutes. Heat wok, add oil, garlic and ginger and stir fry briefly. Add duck and brown all over. Remove duck and set aside. Lower heat and add yellow beans and spring onions and stir fry 2 minutes. Add stock and remainder of marinade and return duck to wok, cover and simmer for 1½ hours, turning and basting the bird every 15 minutes.

When cooked, remove duck and chop into bite-size pieces and arrange on serving dish. Thicken liquid in wok with cornflour mixed with cold water. Bring to the boil and pour over duck. Garnish with fresh coriander sprigs and blanched red and green capsicum shreds.

STIR-FRIED DUCK WITH GINGER

CHINA

Serves: 4

This dish should be made with very young tender ginger at the stage when it is tipped with pink. If using older ginger, reduce the quantity by half.

Half of a 2 kg (4 lb) roasting duck
½ teaspoon salt
½ teaspoon five spice powder
½ tablespoon unbeaten egg white
2 teaspoons cornflour
125 g (4 oz) very young ginger
1 spring onion
1 teaspoon salt
1 teaspoon sugar
3 tablespoons peanut oil
1 teaspoon crushed garlic
2 tablespoons light soy
1 tablespoon Chinese wine or dry
  sherry
½ cup stock
2 teaspoons cornflour
1 tablespoon cold water

Garnish:
spring onions

Bone the duck. Cut the flesh into very thin slices and mix with ½ teaspoon salt, five spice powder, egg white and cornflour. Put the duck bones into a saucepan with just enough water to cover, a slice of ginger and 1 spring onion. Bring to boil, cover and simmer for 20 minutes to make stock. Scrape off skin of ginger with a small knife and slice ginger thinly. Cut slices into very fine shreds, sprinkle with salt and sugar and set aside for 10 minutes, then squeeze out excess liquid.

Heat 2 tablespoons peanut oil in wok and stir fry the duck until it changes colour. Remove to a plate. Heat remaining tablespoon oil in wok and on low heat fry the garlic, stirring, for a few seconds. Add ginger and fry for 1 minute, then return duck to pan and cook for a further 2 minutes.

Add the soy, sherry and stock mixed together and bring to the boil. Stir in cornflour mixed smoothly with cold water and let it boil and thicken. Transfer to serving dish and garnish with spring onion flowers. Serve with steamed rice.

Note: To make spring onion flowers, cut 7.5 cm (3 inch) lengths of spring onions, using green portion as well as white. With a sharp knife fringe the ends. Drop into a bowl of ice-cold water and refrigerate until ends curl.

RED-COOKED DUCK WITH MUSHROOMS

CHINA

Serves: 6

10 dried Chinese mushrooms
1 x 2 kg (4 lb) roasting duck
1 tablespoon finely shredded ginger
2 cloves garlic, chopped finely
3 whole star anise
1 cup soy sauce
1½ cups water
¼ cup Chinese wine or dry sherry
1 tablespoon sugar
1 tablespoon sesame oil

Soak dried mushrooms in hot water for 30 minutes. Cut off and discard the stems. Wash the duck well inside and out and discard any excess fat. Put duck and mushrooms into wok, add ginger, garlic and star anise. Mix together the soy sauce, water, sherry, sugar and half the sesame oil. Pour around duck. Cover and bring slowly to simmering point, simmer for 1½ hours or until duck is tender. Turn duck every 20 minutes or so, basting with the liquid and adding more boiling water if necessary. Allow duck to cool slightly in the liquid. Lift on to board and brush with remaining sesame oil.

Divide duck in half down the centre, then turn each half cut side down on board and chop into bite-size pieces with cleaver.

Reassemble on serving dish, arrange mushrooms around, spoon some of the sauce over and serve with steaming hot white rice.

Remaining sauce may be frozen and used as a master sauce for other red-cooked dishes.

STEAMED DUCK WITH CHINESE CABBAGE

CHINA

Serves: 4

half a 2 kg (4 lb) roasting duck
3 tablespoons light soy
3 tablespoons dry sherry
1 teaspoon sesame oil
1 teaspoon finely grated fresh ginger
3 spring onions cut in bite-size pieces
1 teaspoon sugar
1 small Chinese cabbage
3 teaspoons cornflour
2 tablespoons cold water

Cut the duck with a cleaver into bite-size pieces, chopping through the bones. Rinse in cold water, making sure any small bits of bone are washed away, and pat dry on paper towels. Put duck into a heat-proof dish or bowl and mix with the soy, sherry, sesame oil, ginger, spring onions and sugar. Place dish on steamer rack over boiling water in wok, cover and steam for 1 hour or until duck is tender, adding more boiling water as necessary. Meanwhile, cut cabbage into 5 cm (2 inch) lengths.

Remove pieces of duck to a warm serving plate. Lift out steaming rack and discard water in wok. Put the liquid from the duck into wok, bring to the boil, add Chinese cabbage, cover and simmer for 3 minutes or until cabbage is tender but still crisp. Remove cabbage and place around duck. Thicken the liquid with cornflour mixed with cold water, stirring over medium heat until it boils. Pour over duck and cabbage and serve hot, accompanied by steamed white rice.

BRAISED MANDARIN DUCK

CHINA

Serves: 6-8

1 x 2 kg (4 lb) duck
2 teaspoons salt
4 x 5 cm (2-inch) squares dried
   tangerine peel
1 whole star anise
2 tablespoons dry sherry
2 tablespoons dark soy sauce
1 tablespoon light soy sauce
2 teaspoons sugar
2 teaspoons finely chopped fresh
   ginger
1 teaspoon finely chopped garlic
oil for frying
1 cup water
3 spring onions cut into 5 cm (2
   inch) lengths
1 teaspoon sesame oil
2 chilli flowers for garnish

Clean and dry duck and rub both inside and out with the salt. Soak the tangerine peels and star anise in boiling water to cover for about 10 minutes. Allow to cool then place in jar of blender together with sherry, soy sauces, sugar, ginger and garlic. Blend at high speed, then use this mixture to brush the duck both inside and out. Let it marinate for 1 hour. Drain, reserving marinade.

Heat 4 tablespoons of oil in a wok, and brown the duck all over. Add reserved marinade and water. Cover and braise over medium low heat for 1 hour, turning the duck every 15 minutes. Add ¼ cup warm water to wok if the liquid evaporates.

Ten minutes before serving the duck, add spring onions and sesame oil to the gravy in the wok, and baste the duck all over. Chop the duck into 2.5 cm (1 inch) pieces and place them in a dish. Pour sauce over the duck. Garnish with chilli flowers, and serve with hot white rice.

ŒUFS BROUILLÉS AUX FINES HERBES

FRANCE

Serves: 4

See picture page 74

6 large eggs
2 tablespoons finely chopped fresh
   herbs such as dill, parsley, chives,
   chervil or thyme
½ teaspoon salt
¼ teaspoon white pepper
2 tablespoons butter

Beat eggs until yolks and whites are thoroughly combined, but do not make them frothy. Stir in most of the chopped herbs, leaving just a little for sprinkling over the cooked eggs. Stir in salt and pepper.

Heat the wok on low heat and melt the butter. Pour in the egg mixture and stir constantly with a wooden spoon over low heat until eggs start to set. Do not cook until dry and firm — the eggs should be moist and creamy. Sprinkle with reserved herbs and serve hot with buttered toast points.

SHANGHAI FRIED EGGS

CHINA

Serves: 4

60 g (2 oz) cellophane noodles
oil for frying
3 egg whites
1 canned bamboo shoot, diced
1 x 220 g (7 oz) can crab meat,
   flaked and drained
1 tablespoon dry sherry
¼ cup chicken stock
½ teaspoon sesame oil
1 teaspoon light soy sauce
⅛ teaspoon ground black pepper
4 sprigs of fresh coriander

Heat wok, add 1 cup oil and deep fry cellophane noodles on both sides till crispy and puffed. Remove noodles from wok, drain on kitchen paper and arrange on serving dish.

Beat egg whites till frothy and combine with bamboo shoot, crab meat, sherry, stock, sesame oil, soy sauce and pepper.

Heat wok and add 2 tablespoons oil. When hot, add half the egg mixture and when centre sets, turn over and fry the other side. Remove and place on noodles. Fry rest of egg mixture and arrange on noodles, garnish with sprigs of fresh coriander and serve immediately.

STEAMED EGG CUSTARD WITH SEAFOOD

JAPAN

Serves: 4

4 dried mushrooms
2 tablespoons Japanese soy sauce
1 tablespoon sugar
4 small prawns or 8 slices fish cake
   (kamaboko)
4 fresh oysters

Custard:
4 eggs
2½ cups dashi (see Glossary)
1½ teaspoons salt
1 tablespoon Japanese soy sauce
2 tablespoons sake, mirin or dry
   sherry

Soak mushrooms in hot water 30 minutes, cut off and discard stems and simmer the caps in a small saucepan with ½ cup water, 1 tablespoon of soy and the sugar for 10 minutes. Shell and de-vein prawns.

Custard: Beat eggs, then mix in all other ingredients. When mixture has been poured into cups, carefully skim off the bubbles on the top of the mixture.

Into each custard cup or ramekin put a mushroom, a prawn or 2 slices fish cake, an oyster. Fill cups with custard mixture and place on a rack in a wok with hot water to come 2.5 cm (1 inch) below rack. Cover each cup with foil, pressing it close over the side of the cup. Cover wok with the lid and bring water to the boil. Lower heat and simmer 15 minutes or until set. Serve hot or cold.

Note: If preferred, substitute thinly sliced chicken breast for the seafood. Half a large chicken breast, skin and bones removed, will be required for this quantity.

CHILLI EGGS INDONESIA

Serves: 4

4 eggs
3 tablespoons peanut oil
1 medium onion, finely chopped
½ teaspoon finely chopped garlic
½ teaspoon dried shrimp paste
  (trasi)
1 tablespoon sambal ulek or chilli
  sauce
½ teaspoon laos powder
3 kemiri nuts, finely grated, optional
½ teaspoon salt
¼ teaspoon ground black pepper
3 teaspoons brown sugar
½ cup canned coconut milk
2 teaspoons lemon juice

Hard boil the eggs, stirring them for the first 5 minutes of cooking so that the yolks are centred. Heat wok, add oil and fry onion and garlic until they are soft and golden. Add shrimp paste, sambal ulek, laos and grated nuts and fry for 1 minute, crushing the trasi with the frying spoon. Add salt, pepper, sugar, coconut milk and lemon juice and simmer gently, stirring constantly, until thick and the oil comes to the surface. Add the shelled and halved eggs, spooning the sauce over them. Serve with hot white rice.

BOMBAY SCRAMBLED EGGS INDIA

Serves: 4-6

6 eggs
4 tablespoons milk
1 teaspoon salt
¼ teaspoon ground black pepper
2 tablespoons ghee
5 spring onions, finely chopped
2 fresh chillies, finely chopped
½ teaspoon finely chopped garlic
1 teaspoon finely chopped fresh
  ginger
¼ teaspoon ground turmeric
3 tablespoons chopped fresh
  coriander leaves
¾ teaspoon ground cummin

Garnish:
4 sprigs of fresh coriander leaves

Beat eggs and milk, salt and pepper until well mixed. Heat wok, add ghee and cook the spring onions, chillies, garlic and ginger until soft. Add turmeric and coriander leaves and stir fry for 2 minutes, then add the egg mixture and ground cummin. Cook over low heat, stirring constantly, until the eggs are of a creamy consistency. Turn on to a serving dish and garnish with fresh coriander sprigs.

STEAMED EGG ROLLS

CHINA

Serves: 4

5 eggs
½ teaspoon salt
⅛ teaspoon ground black pepper
2 tablespoons peanut oil
1 teaspoon sesame oil

Filling:
185 g (6 oz) minced lean pork
½ teaspoon salt
¼ teaspoon ground black pepper
1 tablespoon light soy sauce
½ teaspoon sesame oil
1 teaspoon cornflour
3 teaspoons finely chopped fresh coriander
2 spring onions, finely chopped

Beat eggs well with salt and pepper. Reserve a tablespoon of the beaten egg for sealing the egg rolls. Heat wok, add 2 teaspoons of the peanut and sesame oils mixed together, and swirl to coat wok. Pour about 3 tablespoons of the egg mixture into wok and make a thin omelette, cooking it on one side only. Turn onto a plate. Repeat with remaining egg mixture. Portion filling to the number of omelettes made.

Filling: Put pork, salt, pepper and soy sauce into container of electric blender and blend until almost a paste. Turn into a bowl, add the other ingredients and mix well.

Place each omelette on a board, cooked side up, and spread filling almost to the edge, roll up like a Swiss roll and seal edges of omelettes with a little of the reserved beaten egg. Place on a dish lightly oiled with the same oil used for cooking the omelette.

Put dish on a rack in a wok containing water, cover and steam for 15 minutes. Remove from dish, cool slightly, and cut into diagonal slices and serve hot or cold.

EGGS FOO YONG WITH PRAWNS

CHINA

Serves: 4-6

1 cup cooked prawns
6 eggs
1 teaspoon salt
¼ teaspoon ground black pepper
6 spring onions, finely chopped
peanut oil for frying

Sweet Sour Sauce:
1 tablespoon light soy sauce
2 tablespoons Chinese wine or dry sherry
2 tablespoons tomato sauce
1 tablespoon white vinegar
2 tablespoons white sugar
½ cup water
1 tablespoon cornflour
1 tablespoon water

Shell, de-vein and roughly chop the prawns and set aside. Beat eggs with salt and pepper. Mix in the prawns and spring onions, heat wok, add 2 teaspoons oil and swirl to coat wok. Pour in ½ cup of the egg mixture. Cook until brown on underside, turn and cook other side. Remove and keep warm. Repeat with remaining mixture and serve with sweet-sour sauce.

Sweet Sour Sauce: Combine soy sauce, wine, tomato sauce, vinegar, sugar and ½ cup water in a saucepan and stir over medium heat until sugar dissolves. Bring to a boil, then stir in cornflour mixed smoothly with cold water and cook, stirring constantly, until thickened.

MEAT

There are recipes from many countries in this chapter, ranging from kidneys in a delicate cream and mushroom sauce from France, to peppery Beef Stroganoff from Russia. Mainly featured, however, are those wonderful Oriental stir-fried dishes, for in cooking these you will use a wok to best advantage.

For stir-fried dishes meat is always cut in paper-thin slices or thin shreds. If the meat is partially frozen it is firmer to handle and easier to slice thinly.

Since the cooking time is so short, if you are in a hurry you must use beef or pork fillet or at least Scotch fillet or rump. If, however, you are thinking far enough ahead, you can use cheaper cuts. Here's how.

More economical cuts such as round or blade steak or fresh silverside may be substituted for the expensive fillet, but they need a little tenderising before they are cooked. The Chinese method is to shred or slice the meat as required. Then, for a half kilo of meat, dissolve half a teaspoon of bicarbonate of soda in three tablespoons water, mix with salt and other seasonings and knead well until meat absorbs the liquid. Cover and refrigerate for 2-4 hours, or overnight if possible. Proceed with the recipe in the usual way. This method is used in many Chinese restaurants, making cheaper cuts of meat as tender as fillet.

STIR-FRIED BEEF WITH CELLOPHANE NOODLES

KOREA

Serves: 4

See picture page 73

250 g (8 oz) tender steak
1 teaspoon sugar
1 tablespoon soy sauce
2 teaspoons finely chopped spring onion
1 teaspoon finely chopped garlic
1 teaspoon finely chopped fresh ginger
1 teaspoon ground toasted sesame seeds
¼ teaspoon ground black pepper
2 tablespoons sesame oil
60 g (2 oz) cellophane noodles
125 g (4 oz) white Chinese cabbage
125 g (4 oz) canned bamboo shoot
1 medium sized carrot
1 medium sized onion
1 large cucumber
few leaves spinach
peanut oil for stir frying
soy sauce, sugar, salt and pepper to taste

Garnish:
2 eggs

Cut beef into paper-thin strips and marinate in a bowl with a mixture of the sugar, soy sauce, spring onion, garlic, ginger, sesame seeds, pepper and sesame oil.

Soak cellophane noodles in hot water for 20 minutes, then drain and cut into 10 cm (4 inch) lengths. Cut cabbage into thin strips and the bamboo shoot and carrot into matchstick strips. Peel the onion, cut in halves and slice finely. Peel the cucumber, cut in halves lengthways and scoop out seeds, then cut into thin strips. Wash the spinach well, steam until soft and cut into shreds.

Garnish: Separate eggs and beat yolks and whites separately with a fork. Lightly grease a wok with oil, preferably sesame oil, and pour in the beaten yolks. Swirl pan to make a very thin omelette. When set, turn and cook other side. Do not allow to brown. Turn on to a plate. Repeat with egg whites. Cut yellow and white omelettes into fine strips.

Heat a tablespoon of oil and stir fry the vegetables, each one separately, until cooked but still crisp. Remove vegetables to a plate. Heat remaining oil, stir fry the beef and noodles. Mix all together on a large plate, season to taste with soy, sugar, salt and pepper according to taste. Garnish with omelette strips and serve very hot.

Opposite: Ingredients and completed dish — Stir Fried Beef with Cellophane Noodles, recipe this page.

BEEF STROGANOFF RUSSIA

Serves: 4

See picture page 93

500 g (1 lb) fillet or scotch fillet
2 tablespoons seasoned flour
500 g (1 lb) fresh mushrooms
4 tablespoons ghee (clarified butter)
 or 2 tablespoons each butter and
 olive oil
1 large onion, finely chopped
1 clove garlic, crushed
1 cup hot stock or water
salt and freshly ground black pepper
½ cup sour cream
poppy seeds (optional)

Slice steak into paper-thin strips and cut into bite-size lengths. Toss in seasoned flour. Wipe over and slice mushrooms.

Heat half the ghee in a wok and stir fry onion and garlic over low heat until onion is soft. Add mushrooms and continue cooking until mushrooms are soft. Remove from wok.

Heat remaining ghee in wok, and on high heat stir fry beef until brown. Add stock, stir well. Return fried onions and mushrooms to wok, season with salt and pepper to taste. Simmer for a few minutes, then stir in sour cream and heat through without boiling. Serve with hot buttered rice or noodles. If liked, sprinkle poppy seeds over buttered noodles and toss.

STIR-FRIED BEEF IN OYSTER SAUCE CHINA

Serves: 4

500 g (1 lb) lean beef
2 tablespoons dark soy sauce
2 tablespoons Chinese wine or dry
 sherry
2 teaspoons chilli sauce
125 g (4 oz) cellophane noodles
2 tablespoons oil
1 teaspoon finely chopped garlic
1 teaspoon finely chopped fresh
 ginger
½ cup stock or hot water
2 teaspoons cornflour
2 tablespoons cold water
2 tablespoons oyster sauce
4 spring onions cut in 2.5 cm (1
 inch) lengths

Slice the lean beef very thinly against the grain. Combine soy sauce, wine and chilli sauce in a bowl and mix well with the beef. Let it marinate while preparing cellophane noodles. Soak the cellophane noodles in hot water for 5 minutes, then boil for 10 minutes. Drain and set aside.

Heat wok, add oil, and when hot fry garlic and ginger for 10 seconds. Add beef and stir fry for 2 minutes or until colour changes. Add stock and rest of the marinade and bring to the boil. Now add cornflour mixed smoothly with the cold water and return to the boil, stirring constantly. Stir until liquid thickens, about 1 minute. Stir in oyster sauce and spring onions and mix well with beef.

Chop cellophane noodles into bite-size lengths and place on a serving dish. Top with beef in oyster sauce and serve immediately.

Opposite: Ingredients for Oeufs Brouillés aux Fines Herbes, recipe page 67.

CHILLI BEEF WITH SHRIMP PASTE

INDONESIA

Serves: 4

500 g (1 lb) topside or round steak
3 tablespoons peanut oil
1 large onion, finely chopped
2 teaspoons finely chopped garlic
2 teaspoons sambal ulek or 3 fresh red
    chillies, seeded and finely chopped
1 teaspoon dried shrimp paste (trasi)
2 teaspoons finely chopped lemon
    rind
2 tablespoons dark soy sauce
¼ cup stock
2 teaspoons palm sugar or substitute

Place the meat, trimmed of all fat, into a saucepan with enough water to cover. Bring to the boil, and simmer for 15 minutes. Allow meat to cool in the stock. When cool enough to handle, slice meat into thin strips.

Heat peanut oil in a wok and fry onion over low heat until soft and transparent. When onion starts to turn golden add garlic, chillies, shrimp paste and lemon rind. Crush shrimp paste in the wok, using the back of a wooden spoon, and stir fry for 1 minute. Add beef and stir fry for about 3–4 minutes on medium heat. Add soy sauce, stock and sugar, stir and continue to cook on low heat until liquid has almost evaporated and oil separates from the rest of the gravy. The oil should have a reddish colour from the chillies. Serve hot with boiled rice and vegetables.

HEARTY BEEF GOULASH

HUNGARY

Serves: 4-6

2 tablespoons lard or oil
1 large onion, finely chopped
1 teaspoon finely chopped garlic
2 tablespoons paprika
750 g (1½ lb) beef, cut into cubes
3 cups beef stock or water
1½ teaspoons salt
½ teaspoon freshly ground black
    pepper
1 cup peeled tomatoes, chopped
1 red or green capsicum
2 medium potatoes
sprinkling of caraway seeds, optional
½ cup sour cream
1 tablespoon tomato paste

Heat the lard or oil and fry the onion and garlic over gentle heat, stirring, until soft and pale golden. Remove wok from heat and stir in the paprika. Add beef, hot stock or water, salt and pepper and return to heat. Bring to simmering point, cover wok and cook for an hour or until beef is almost tender.

While beef is cooking, prepare the tomatoes, capsicum and potatoes. Canned tomatoes may be used. Chop the capsicum finely, discarding seeds and membrane.

Peel the potatoes, cut into large cubes and cook them in boiling salted water until half cooked. Drain. Add the vegetables to the pan together with caraway seeds if used. Stir well, and if necessary add a little more hot stock or water to wok. Cover and continue cooking for a further 15-20 minutes until potatoes and meat are completely cooked. Stir in sour cream and tomato paste and serve hot.

STIR-FRIED BEEF IN BLACK BEAN SAUCE

CHINA

Serves: 4

2 tablespoons canned salted black
 beans
2 tablespoons Chinese wine or dry
 sherry
¼ cup stock or water
1 teaspoon sugar
2 teaspoons cornflour
1 tablespoon cold water
2 tablespoons peanut oil
1 teaspoon sesame oil
375 g (¾ lb) lean beef, topside or
 blade, thinly sliced (see
 Introduction to Meat Chapter,
 p.71)
1 teaspoon finely chopped garlic
2 tablespoons chopped spring onions

Garnish:
1 red chilli flower

Put black beans into a strainer and rinse under cold water for a few seconds. Drain, then mash with a fork, and combine with the wine, water and sugar. Mix cornflour with cold water and set aside.

Heat wok, add both oils and swirl to coat the wok. Add beef and fry over high heat, tossing and stirring constantly until beef loses its redness. Move beef to side of wok and add garlic and spring onions and stir fry for a minute longer, then add bean mixture. Bring to the boil, add cornflour mixture, and stir till sauce thickens. Draw in meat and mix with sauce. Serve hot garnished with chilli flower and accompanied by hot white rice.

STIR-FRIED BEEF WITH VEGETABLES

CHINA

Serves: 4

375 g (12 oz) lean steak
1 tablespoon soy sauce
½ teaspoon crushed garlic
½ teaspoon sesame oil
1 teaspoon finely grated fresh ginger
2 tablespoons soy sauce
1 teaspoon sugar
1 teaspoon chilli bean sauce, optional
¼ cup stock or water
½ cup celery, cut in julienne strips
½ cup bamboo shoot, cut in julienne
   strips
1 medium onion, sliced finely and
   separated in layers
2 tablespoons peanut oil
1 teaspoon cornflour mixed with 2
   teaspoons cold water

Cooking for guests as they watch always adds an extra dimension to any meal and when it is a dish that happens as quickly as this one, they will applaud the apparently magical way you create a dish in minutes. You, of course, will be applauding the wok. Have the beef marinated, the seasoning mixed in a small bowl, the vegetables ready sliced, the cornflour and water combined in a separate container. It will take hardly five minutes to cook the dish. And have ready a bowl of hot cooked rice for eating with the beef.

Slice the beef thinly against the grain and cut into bite-size lengths. Mix steak with 1 tablespoon soy sauce, crushed garlic and sesame oil. In a small bowl combine the ginger, remaining 2 tablespoons soy sauce, sugar, chilli bean sauce (if a hot flavour is desired) and stock or water. Stir to dissolve sugar. Have ready the vegetables in a bowl, and the cornflour combined with water.

When ready to cook, heat 1 tablespoon peanut oil in wok until very hot, swirl wok to coat sides with oil. Add vegetables and stir fry on high heat for 2 minutes. Remove to a dish. Heat the remaining tablespoon of oil, add beef and fry on high heat until colour changes, tossing and stirring constantly. Push beef to side of wok. Add mixed seasoning ingredients, bring to the boil, then stir in the cornflour and cook, stirring, until it clears and thickens. Return beef and vegetables to the sauce and heat through. Turn off heat and serve immediately, directly from the wok, accompanied by hot cooked rice.

STIR-FRIED BEEF WITH CAULIFLOWER

CHINA

Serves: 4

1 cup cauliflower sprigs
1 tablespoon oil
½ teaspoon finely chopped garlic
½ teaspoon finely chopped fresh
  ginger
¾ cup spring onions, cut into 2.5 cm
  (1 inch) lengths
375 g (¾ lb) beef, topside or blade,
  thinly sliced (see Introduction to
  Meat Chapter, p.71)
1 tablespoon dark soy sauce
½ cup hot water
¼ teaspoon ground black pepper
1 tablespoon hoi sin sauce
2 teaspoons cornflour
1 tablespoon cold water
salt to taste

Garnish:
4 red chilli flowers

Blanch cauliflower sprigs in boiling water for 1 minute, drain and refresh under running cold water. Set aside. Heat wok, add oil and when hot add garlic and ginger and stir fry for 1 minute. Add cauliflower sprigs and spring onions and stir fry 1 minute and move to the side of the wok.

Raise heat, add beef and stir fry till colour changes then move up the side of wok. Add soy sauce, hot water, pepper, hoi sin, then add mixture of cornflour and cold water. Stir till sauce thickens, draw in meat and vegetables and mix with sauce. Serve hot garnished with chilli flowers.

Note: To make chilli flowers split fresh chillies from tip to within half-inch of stalk and soak in iced water in refrigerator for at least one hour or until 'petals' curl.

STIR-FRIED BEEF WITH RED CAPSICUMS

CHINA

Serves: 4

375 g (¾ lb) beef, topside or blade, thinly sliced (see Introduction to Meat Chapter, p.71)
1 medium onion
3 tablespoons peanut oil
¼ cup cashews
1 teaspoon finely chopped garlic
½ teaspoon finely chopped fresh ginger
1 cup 2.5 cm (1 inch) diced red capsicums
1 tablespoon dark soy sauce
2 tablespoons Chinese wine or dry sherry
1 teaspoon cornflour
2 tablespoons cold water
salt to taste

Garnish:
spring onion flowers

Partially freeze the meat to assist in slicing thinly, then marinate to tenderize as described on page 71. Peel onion, cut in quarters lengthways and halves across. Separate the layers and set aside. Heat wok, add 1 tablespoon of oil and fry cashews golden brown and set aside. Add remaining oil to wok, heat, and stir fry garlic and ginger for 1 minute. Add capsicum and onions, stir, cover and simmer for 2 minutes. Move vegetables up the side of wok.

Raise heat, add meat and stir fry till colour changes. Add soy sauce and wine and stir the meat with all the vegetables. Mix cornflour with cold water, add to wok and stir till sauce thickens. Serve garnished with spring onion flowers and cashews.

RED-STEWED BEEF

CHINA

Serves: 4-6

2 tablespoons peanut oil
1 kg (2 lb) beef shin (gravy beef) in one piece
¼ teaspoon pepper
1 teaspoon finely chopped fresh ginger
1 teaspoon finely chopped garlic
1 spring onion, cut in two pieces
2 tablespoons sugar
¾ cup dark soy sauce
1 teaspoon sesame oil
¼ cup Chinese wine or dry sherry
2 whole star anise
boiling water

Heat wok, add oil and raise heat fully. Add meat and brown on all sides. Add all other ingredients and enough boiling water to cover the meat. Bring to the boil, then turn heat low to simmer gently. Cover and simmer for 2½ hours, turning meat in the sauce every 30 minutes. Test beef by piercing with a skewer — it should penetrate easily. Transfer to a bowl and allow the beef to cool in the sauce, turning it over from time to time. Remove beef and cut into very thin slices and serve with hot white rice or serve cold as hors d'oeuvres.

Note: Save the master sauce, as the cooking liquid is now called, and freeze it for future use. A spoonful added to a dish will give a rich delicious flavour.

SHREDDED CHILLI BEEF   CHINA—SZECHWAN

Serves: 4

500 g (1 lb) lean beef
2 tablespoons Chinese wine or dry
    sherry
1 tablespoon dark soy sauce
2 tablespoons preserved radish with
    chilli, chopped, or 2 teaspoons
    chilli sauce
1 tablespoon cornflour
½ cup stock or cold water
2 tablespoons peanut oil
2 teaspoons finely chopped garlic
2 teaspoons finely chopped fresh
    ginger
4 tablespoons finely chopped spring
    onions
½ cup canned bamboo shoot,
    shredded
½ cup fresh red chillies, seeded and
    shredded

Cut the beef into very thin slices and then shred finely. Mix together wine, soy sauce, chopped radish and set aside. Mix together cornflour and stock and set aside.

Heat wok, add oil and when hot add garlic, ginger and spring onions. Raise heat and stir fry 1 minute. Add shredded beef and stir fry 1 minute. Add shredded bamboo shoot and chillies and stir fry 1 minute longer. Add wine, soy, radish mixture and bring to the boil. Add cornflour and stock mixture, stir till liquid thickens and serve with hot white rice.

SHREDDED BEEF WITH HOT
SESAME SAUCE   VIETNAM

Serves: 2-3

375 g (12 oz) rump steak
3 tablespoons peanut oil
1 teaspoon finely chopped garlic
2 tablespoons dark soy sauce
½ cup beef stock
3 teaspoons cornflour
2 tablespoons cold water
1 tablespoon sesame paste
1 table Chinese chilli
    sauce

Garnish:
3 tablespoons chopped fresh
    coriander

Shred rump steak into very thin strips. Heat peanut oil in a wok, add garlic and meat and stir fry over high heat until meat has changed colour, about 2 minutes. Add soy sauce and stock and bring to the boil, then stir in cornflour mixed smoothly with cold water, stirring until it boils and thickens. Turn off heat, stir in sesame paste and chilli sauce. Garnish with fresh coriander and serve with hot white rice.

81

BRAISED BEEF SHORTRIBS WITH SESAME SAUCE

KOREA

Serves: 4

1.5 kg (3 lb) shortribs of beef
1 tablespoon peanut oil
2 tablespoons dark soy sauce
2 teaspoons sesame oil
4 spring onions, finely chopped
1 teaspoon finely chopped garlic
1 teaspoon finely chopped fresh
    ginger
2 tablespoons sugar
3 tablespoons rice wine or dry sherry
2 tablespoons toasted, ground sesame
    seeds
2 cups hot water
1 teaspoon cornflour
1 tablespoon cold water
spring onion flowers
few sprigs fresh coriander leaves,
    optional

You can buy the ribs already cut into short lengths at many supermarkets, or ask your butcher to chop spareribs across into short lengths of about 5 cm (2 inches). Separate them with a sharp cleaver, heat oil in a wok and brown the ribs over high heat. Combine all other ingredients (except cornflour and cold water) and add to wok, bring to the boil, then cover and simmer 50-60 minutes or until tender. Add cornflour mixed with cold water and stir constantly over medium heat until gravy boils and thickens. Garnish with spring onion flowers and if liked, sprigs of fresh coriander and serve with hot white rice.

To make spring onion flowers, cut into short lengths and split one or both ends several times with a sharp knife. Soak in iced water for a few minutes until the ends curl.

KIDNEYS WITH MUSHROOMS AND CREAM SAUCE

FRANCE

Serves: 4

8 lambs' kidneys or 2 veal kidneys
60 g (2 oz) butter
salt and freshly ground pepper
3 tablespoons cognac or brandy
250 g (8 oz) button mushrooms,
    sliced
3 spring onions, finely chopped
1 teaspoon fresh or ½ teaspoon dried
    thyme
½ cup stock
¼ cup Madeira or dry French
    vermouth
½ cup cream
2 teaspoons prepared French mustard

Cut the kidneys in halves lengthways. Remove and discard core and cut kidneys in thick slices. Heat half the butter in wok, add the kidneys and saute, stirring, for about 8 minutes. Season well with salt and pepper.

Heat the cognac in a brandy warmer or small saucepan or ladle, pour over the kidneys and ignite. Shake the pan or baste kidneys with a long-handled spoon until flames subside.

Transfer contents of wok to a dish, cover and keep warm. Wipe out wok with kitchen paper.

Heat remaining butter and on low heat fry the mushrooms and spring onions, stirring, for 3 or 4 minutes. Add the thyme, stock, wine and cream and bring to simmering point. Stir in the mustard. Return the kidneys and heat through without boiling. Serve immediately with toast points, sauteed potatoes or steamed rice.

TRIPE ITALIENNE

ITALY

Serves: 4-6

See picture page 92

60 g (2 oz) butter
4 tablespoons olive oil
3 medium onions, chopped
1 teaspoon finely chopped garlic
1 stick celery, chopped
4 bay leaves
1 x 250 g (8 oz) can champignons, sliced
1 kg (2 lb) honeycomb tripe, cut into bite-size squares
2 tablespoons tomato paste
1 cup beef stock
½ cup Moselle wine
1 teaspoon salt
½ teaspoon ground black pepper
¼ cup fresh cream
60 g (2 oz) grated Parmesan cheese

Garnish:
½ cup sliced pimiento olives
finely chopped parsley

Heat butter and oil in wok, add onions, stir on medium heat till onions start to brown. Add garlic, celery, bay leaves and mushrooms, stir for 2 minutes, add tripe, tomato paste, stock, wine, salt and pepper. Raise heat and stir thoroughly. Lower heat, cover wok and simmer for 1 hour or until tender, stirring every 15 minutes.

When tripe is cooked, stir in the cream and turn on to serving dish. Sprinkle with cheese and garnish with parsley and sliced olives.

VEAL SAUTÉ WITH MUSHROOMS

SWITZERLAND

Serves: 4

500 g (1 lb) veal steaks sliced 6 mm
 (¼ inch) thick
¾ teaspoon salt
½ teaspoon pepper
plain flour
2 tablespoons butter
2 tablespoons olive oil
500 g (1 lb) button mushrooms,
 sliced
3 tablespoons finely chopped spring
 onions
1 teaspoon finely chopped garlic
½ cup dry white wine
½ cup thick cream
extra salt and pepper to taste

Garnish:
finely chopped parsley

Sprinkle veal steaks with salt and pepper, dust with flour and set aside. Heat half the butter and olive oil in wok and saute veal for 4 minutes. Remove veal from wok on to warmed serving dish and reserve pan juices in a separate bowl. Heat remaining butter and olive oil in wok, add mushrooms and stir fry till brown. Now add garlic and spring onions and stir fry for two minutes longer, then add the wine. Simmer for another 5 minutes. Add the cream and stir 1 minute then add pan juices and adjust seasoning. Return veal strips to wok to reheat without boiling. Transfer to serving dish and garnish with chopped parsley. Serve with buttered noodles.

MONGOLIAN LAMB

CHINA

Serves: 4-6

1 kg (2 lb) boned leg of lamb
1 tablespoon sugar
1 teaspoon salt
2 tablespoons dark soy sauce
1 egg
¼ teaspoon bicarbonate of soda
15 g (1 oz) cornflour
4 tablespoons peanut oil
1 teaspoon finely chopped garlic
1 spring onion, finely sliced
¼ teaspoon five spice powder
1 heaped tablespoon hoi sin sauce
1 teaspoon bean sauce (mor sze
 jeung)
1 tablespoon dry sherry

Trim away all fat, skin and gristle and cut the lean meat into bite-size, paper-thin slices. Soak in cold water for 30 minutes. Rinse until water runs clear, then drain well and squeeze out excess water. Add sugar, salt, soy sauce, egg, bicarbonate of soda (for tenderising) and cornflour. Mix well, then add 1 tablespoon of the peanut oil and mix again. Leave to marinate at least 2 hours.

Heat a wok, add 2 tablespoons peanut oil, and on very high heat stir fry the lamb until colour changes. Remove lamb from wok. Heat remaining 1 tablespoon oil over low heat, add garlic and spring onion and cook gently until they start to colour. Add the five spice powder, hoi sin sauce and bean sauce, return lamb to wok, and toss over high heat. Add sherry, mix and serve at once.

BRAISED PORK WITH BLACK BEANS

SINGAPORE

Serves: 4-6

750 g (1½ lb) loin of pork (rind and bone removed)
2 teaspoons finely chopped garlic
1 teaspoon finely chopped fresh ginger
2 tablespoons Chinese wine or dry sherry
½ teaspoon five spice powder
2 tablespoons black beans, chopped
1 tablespoon chilli sauce
1 tablespoon peanut oil
hot water or stock
1 red capsicum 2.5 cm (1 inch) diced
5 spring onions cut into 2.5 cm (1 inch) lengths

Cut pork into strips 5 cm (2 inches) long and 2.5 cm (1 inch) wide. Combine garlic, ginger, Chinese wine, five spice powder, black beans, chilli sauce and rub over the pork. Set aside to marinate for 20 minutes. Heat wok, add oil and swirl to coat wok. Add the pork pieces, reserving marinade. Stir fry the pork over high heat until browned, then add reserved marinade, washing out the bowl with half cup hot water and adding that to wok.

Reduce heat, cover and simmer for 40 minutes until pork is tender. Stir occasionally and add more hot water if liquid looks like drying up. Ten minutes before serving, add capsicum and spring onions and mix through the pork. Serve with hot boiled rice.

PORK WITH BRAISED SPINACH

KOREA

Serves: 4

1 bunch fresh spinach
250 g (8 oz) pork shoulder
2 tablespoons peanut oil
1 teaspoon finely chopped garlic
2 tablespoons light soy sauce
¼ teaspoon ground black pepper
1 cup diced canned bamboo shoot
5 spring onions, finely chopped
½ teaspoon sesame oil
3 tablespoons toasted, crushed sesame seeds

Wash spinach well, remove tough stem and break leaves into large pieces. Dice the pork very small. Heat wok, add oil and when hot fry the pork and garlic, stirring constantly, until pork changes colour. Add spinach and toss well, season with soy sauce and pepper. Cover and simmer on low heat until pork is tender. Add bamboo shoot, spring onions, egg and sesame oil and stir well over medium heat for 2 minutes. Sprinkle with sesame seeds and serve hot with rice.

STIR-FRIED PORK WITH CELLOPHANE NOODLES

CHINA

Serves: 4

125 g (4 oz) cellophane noodles
6 dried Chinese mushrooms
250 g (8 oz) pork
2 tablespoons Chinese wine or dry
  sherry
1 tablespoon light soy sauce
1 teaspoon salt
1 cup stock or mushroom liquid
1 teaspoon cornflour
3 tablespoons peanut oil
5 spring onions, finely chopped
2 teaspoons finely chopped fresh
  ginger
2 tablespoons chilli bean sauce
2 fresh red chillies, seeded and finely
  chopped
4 tablespoons chopped fresh
  coriander leaves

Put the noodles in a large bowl, pour over boiling water to cover, and leave to soak 10 minutes. Strain noodles and cut into short lengths and set aside. Soak mushrooms in hot water for 30 minutes, squeeze dry, cut off and discard stems, dice caps finely and reserve soaking water. Cut pork into paper-thin, bite-size strips. Mix wine, soy, salt, stock and cornflour together in a small bowl and set aside.

Heat wok, add oil and swirl around wok. When oil is hot, add the pork and mushrooms and stir fry until cooked and brown. Add spring onions and ginger, stir fry for 1 minute, then add bean sauce and red chillies and cook over medium heat for 2 minutes.

Add the sauce mixture and stir until it comes to the boil, then add noodles and simmer, stirring until liquid is reduced. Stir in coriander leaves and serve at once.

STEAMED MARINATED PORK

CHINA

Serves: 6

1 kg (2 lb) lean belly pork
4 tablespoons dark soy sauce
3 tablespoons Chinese wine or dry
  sherry
½ teaspoon five spice powder
1 teaspoon crushed garlic
½ cup uncooked rice

Ask your butcher to remove skin from pork. Cut pork into 5 cm (2 inch) squares and marinate in a mixture of soy sauce, wine, five spice powder and garlic for at least an hour.

Roast uncooked rice in a wok on low heat, stirring constantly, until the grains turn golden in colour. Cool, and put into container of electric blender and blend on high speed until ground to powder.

Roll pieces of pork, one at a time, in the rice powder and put them into a heatproof dish. Place on steaming rack in wok and steam over boiling water for 2 hours, adding more boiling water as necessary, until the pork is tender enough to be broken with chopsticks. Serve hot, accompanied by steamed white rice.

FRIED PORK WITH SWEET-SOUR SAUCE

CHINA

Serves: 4-6

500 g (1 lb) pork fillet
1 tablespoon light soy sauce
1 tablespoon Chinese wine or dry
**   sherry**
½ teaspoon salt
¼ teaspoon pepper
¼ teaspoon five spice powder
1 cup plain flour
¾ cup warm water
1 tablespoon peanut oil
1 egg white
extra peanut oil for frying

Sweet-Sour Sauce:
1 tablespoon light soy sauce
2 tablespoons Chinese wine or dry
**   sherry**
3 tablespoons tomato sauce
1 tablespoon white vinegar
2 tablespoons white sugar
½ cup water
1 tablespoon cornflour
1 tablespoon water
1 small onion
2 tablespoons peanut oil
1 clove garlic, crushed
¼ teaspoon finely grated fresh ginger
2 tablespoons preserved melon
**   shreds**

Cut pork into 12 mm (½ inch) slices, then into 2.5 cm (1 inch) squares. Mix with soy sauce, wine, salt, pepper and five spice powder. Refrigerate while preparing batter.

Mix flour and warm water to a smooth batter with a wooden spoon, stir in oil and allow to stand for 30 minutes. Beat egg white until stiff and fold in. Heat wok and add oil. When oil is hot, dip pieces of pork in batter and deep fry a few at a time over medium heat, until pork is cooked and batter golden. Drain on kitchen paper and set aside. Make sauce.

Sweet-Sour Sauce: Combine soy sauce, wine, tomato sauce, vinegar, sugar and water in a bowl and stir until sugar dissolves.

Mix cornflour smoothly with about 1 tablespoon cold water. Peel onion, cut into four lengthways, then cut each quarter across into two. Separate layers of onion. Heat oil, add garlic, ginger and fry for 1 minute. Add combined sauce mixture, bring to a boil, then stir in cornflour and cook, stirring constantly, until thickened. Remove from heat, stir in melon shreds.

Shortly before serving, reheat oil and once more fry pork, a few pieces at a time, on high heat for just a few seconds. This second frying makes the batter very crisp. Drain on kitchen paper and set aside. When all the pork is fried, arrange on a serving dish, pour hot sauce over and serve immediately, with hot white rice.

VEGETABLES

RATATOUILLE NIÇOISE   FRANCE

Serves: 4-6

See picture page 91

Ratatouille Niçoise is a vegetable medley to accompany meat or poultry. It can also be served by itself as a separate course with crusty bread. It may be served hot or at room temperature, and is one of the few vegetable dishes that is not spoiled when prepared ahead and reheated.

1 medium eggplant
2 zucchini
2 medium onions
2 large ripe tomatoes
1 red capsicum
1 green capsicum
1 teaspoon finely chopped garlic
¼ cup olive oil
1½ teaspoons salt
¼ teaspoon freshly ground black
    pepper
1 tablespoon chopped fresh basil or 1
    teaspoon dried basil
2 bay leaves

Wash but do not peel eggplant and zucchini. Cut eggplant into dice, sprinkle liberally with salt and set aside for 1 hour, then press out all the excess liquid. Dice zucchini. Slice onions finely. Peel and chop tomatoes, discarding seeds as much as possible. Remove seeds and membranes from capsicums and dice or slice finely.

Heat olive oil in wok and on medium low heat fry the onions, stirring, until they are soft but not brown. Add the eggplant, zucchini, tomatoes, capsicums and garlic. Add seasonings and herbs. Stir well, turn heat very low and simmer, covered, for 25-30 minutes, stirring occasionally to ensure mixture does not stick at bottom of wok. Vegetables should be soft but not cooked to a pulp. If you have cooked this dish before in a conventional pan, you will find that in a wok the vegetables cook in much less time. Serve warm or at room temperature.

GREEN BEANS WITH GARLIC AND TOMATOES
ITALY

Serves: 4-5

See picture page 91

500 g (1 lb) tender green beans
2-3 tablespoons olive oil
1 teaspoon crushed garlic
½ cup fresh or canned tomatoes, seeded and chopped
2 teaspoons tomato paste
1 teaspoon dried oregano or 1 tablespoon fresh oregano
2 tablespoons finely grated Parmesan, optional

Top and tail the beans, remove any strings and slice diagonally or cut into bite-size lengths. Cook in lightly salted boiling water in a covered wok for about 8 minutes or until just tender. Drain in colander and refresh in cold water to set the colour and stop beans cooking further.

Heat olive oil in wok and on low heat fry the garlic for a few seconds. Do not let it brown. Add the tomatoes, tomato paste and oregano, cover and cook for a few minutes until tomatoes are pulpy. Stir in the beans and toss just to heat through and coat with the tomato mixture. Serve at once, sprinkled with the grated Parmesan.

HONEY GLAZED MUSHROOMS
CHINA

Serves: 4

See picture page 91

500 g (1 lb) fresh young mushrooms
1 tablespoon peanut oil
1 tablespoon honey
2 tablespoons soy sauce

Wipe mushrooms clean and trim stalks level with caps. Heat oil in wok and swirl so that oil coats inside of wok. Add mushrooms and stir fry for 1 minute over medium high heat. Add honey and soy sauce, turn heat low, cover and cook for about 3 minutes. Uncover and cook until liquid thickens, turning mushrooms in the honey and soy mixture to coat them. Serve hot or cold as an accompaniment to other dishes or as a side dish with barbecued meats.

SPICY FRIED GREEN BEANS   INDIA

Serves: 4

500 g (1 lb) tender green beans
2 tablespoons oil
1 medium onion, finely sliced
1 teaspoon finely chopped fresh
   ginger
½ teaspoon ground turmeric
½ teaspoon chilli powder
1 teaspoon salt
1 large ripe tomato, diced
½ cup hot water
½ teaspoon garam masala (see
   Glossary)

Top and tail the beans, removing any strings. Cut them into bite-size lengths. Heat the oil in a wok and on medium heat fry the onion, stirring frequently, until it is soft. Add the ginger and fry for a further minute or two, then add turmeric, chilli powder and salt. Add beans and toss to mix well, then add the diced tomato and hot water and bring to the boil. Cover and cook on low heat for about 10 minutes or until beans are just tender. Sprinkle with garam masala, mix well and cook for a minute longer. Serve with rice.

SPICY CAULIFLOWER AND NUTS   INDIA

Serves: 4

1 cup raw peanuts
½ cup raw cashews
half a small cauliflower
¼ cup oil
1 teaspoon black mustard seeds
1 medium onion, finely chopped
1 teaspoon finely chopped garlic
½ teaspoon finely chopped fresh
   ginger
½ teaspoon ground turmeric
1 teaspoon ground cummin
½ teaspoon salt or to taste
¼ cup hot water
3 tablespoons fresh coriander leaves,
   chopped

Soak the nuts in water overnight. Next day boil them for 10 minutes, then drain well. Separate the cauliflower into sprigs or cut into thick slices, keeping a bit of the stem on each.

Heat oil in a wok and fry the mustard seeds and onion, stirring frequently, until the mustard pops and onion is soft. Add garlic and ginger and fry for a few seconds longer, stirring, then add turmeric and cummin, add nuts and toss together. Sprinkle with salt, add cauliflower and stir well. Add ¼ cup hot water, cover with lid and simmer on low heat for 5 minutes. Uncover and raise heat to evaporate excess liquid, stirring frequently. Taste and add salt if required. Serve hot, sprinkled with the chopped coriander.

This may be an accompaniment to rice as part of a meal, or it can be treated as a light luncheon dish in itself.

Opposite: Ratatouille Nicoise, recipe page 88, Green Beans with Garlic and Tomatoes, recipe page 89, and Honey Glazed Mushrooms, recipe page 89.
Next page: Tripe Italienne, recipe page 83.
Page 93: Beef Stroganoff, recipe page 75.

MIXED BRAISED VEGETABLES   CHINA

Serves: 4

2 tablespoons peanut oil
1 clove garlic, crushed
1 teaspoon finely grated fresh ginger
1 cup finely sliced celery
1 cup sliced red and green capsicums
1 cup sliced Chinese cabbage or
   broccoli
6 spring onions cut into bite-size
   lengths
½ cup stock or water
1 tablespoon light soy sauce
½ teaspoon salt
2 teaspoons cornflour
1 tablespoon cold water

Heat oil in wok and on low heat fry the garlic and ginger for a few seconds, stirring. Do not brown. Add all the vegetables and stir fry for 2 minutes on high heat, then add stock or water, soy sauce and salt. Lower heat, cover and cook for a further 3 minutes. Mix cornflour smoothly with cold water. Push vegetables to side of wok, stir cornflour into liquid and cook, stirring constantly, until it boils and thickens. Toss vegetables in sauce and serve with steamed rice.

Note: Canned bamboo shoots, water chestnuts and baby corn make good additions to the fresh vegetables. Cut bamboo shoot in slices or strips and slice the water chestnuts before adding to dish.

ZUCCHINI IN GARLIC BUTTER   ITALY

Serves: 4

2 or 3 large zucchini
1 tablespoon olive oil
60 g (2 oz) butter
1 teaspoon crushed garlic
salt and freshly ground black pepper

Wash zucchini, trim off stem ends and shred coarsely on grater in food processor.
   Heat oil, butter and garlic in wok on low heat, add the zucchini and toss to mix. Season with salt and pepper, cover and cook on medium low heat for about 3 minutes, just until tender. Serve hot.

Opposite: Chicken and Pork Fried Rice, recipe page 99.

BROCCOLI IN CREAM SAUCE   FRANCE

Serves: 4

500 g (1 lb) broccoli
1 cup chicken stock or water and
    stock cube
½ cup cream or evaporated milk
3 teaspoons cornflour
1 tablespoon cold water

Divide broccoli into sprigs and peel stalks if necessary. Slit any thick stems to speed cooking. Bring the chicken stock to a boil in the wok. Place broccoli in the wok with stems in the stock but the flower heads above the liquid. Cover and steam on medium low heat for 7 or 8 minutes.

Gently lift broccoli to serving dish. Add cream or milk to stock and return to the boil. Mix cornflour smoothly with cold water. Away from heat, stir into liquid. Return to low heat and cook, stirring constantly, until sauce thickens. Season with salt and pepper, pour over the broccoli and serve hot.

BUTTERED SCALLOPINI   ITALY

Serves: 4

500 g (1 lb) scallopini or miniature
    squash
salt and pepper
60 g (2 oz) butter
1 clove garlic, crushed

Wash the scallopini, top and tail them and put on steamer rack above boiling water in wok. Cover and steam for 8-10 minutes or until tender when pierced with a skewer. Do not let them cook too long or they will be soft and mushy. Remove to a dish.

Pour off water and dry the wok well. Add butter and melt over low heat. Add crushed garlic and stir until golden, not letting it brown. Add the scallopini and toss over low heat until heated through. Season to taste with salt and pepper and serve hot.

SAUTÉED MUSHROOMS WITH
BACON   U.S.A.

Serves: 4

500 g (1 lb) small mushrooms
125 g (4 oz) bacon
90 g (3 oz) butter
pepper and salt

Wipe over the mushrooms with a damp paper towel. Remove rind and chop bacon. Heat butter in wok, add bacon and fry until fat is transparent. Add the mushrooms and toss and fry for 4 or 5 minutes. Season with salt and pepper to taste. Serve hot, as an accompaniment to meat or poultry.

96

BRAISED CELERY AMANDINE   FRANCE

Serves: 4

6-8 stalks celery
30 g (1 oz) butter
1 tablespoon oil
¼ cup slivered almonds
½ cup light stock or water
¼ cup cream
pepper and salt

String celery and cut into sections about 7.5 cm (3 inches) in length. Heat butter and oil in wok and on medium low heat fry the almonds, stirring, until golden brown. Remove almonds from pan. Add celery and saute until lightly coloured, then add stock, season with pepper and salt, cover and simmer for 8-10 minutes or until celery is tender but still crisp.

Remove celery to warm serving dish, add cream to pan and heat through, reducing the sauce if it is too thick or, if liked, using a teaspoon of cornflour mixed with cold water to thicken. Pour over the celery, sprinkle with almonds and serve hot.

STEAMED CAULIFLOWER À LA POLONAISE   FRANCE

Serves: 4-6

60 g (2 oz) butter
½ cup soft white breadcrumbs
1 firm white cauliflower
1 cup water
salt
1 hard boiled egg
2 tablespoons finely chopped parsley

A wok is ideal to cook those large, perfect cauliflowers that are too big for the average pan. Even when you have a large saucepan into which you can fit the cauliflower it is almost impossible to lift this vegetable out of any saucepan without breaking it when it is cooked. The wide, flaring shape of the wok makes the task very simple.

Melt butter in the wok and on low heat toss the breadcrumbs in butter until golden. Remove to a plate and reserve. Trim cauliflower and make two slits in the stem with a sharp knife. Put a cup of water in the wok. Add a little salt, bring to the boil. Place cauliflower in wok so stem end is in the water. Cover with lid and steam for about 8 minutes or until just tender. A very large cauliflower may require longer.

Lift carefully from wok and drain. Place on heated serving dish and sprinkle buttered crumbs over. Push yolk of hard boiled egg through a sieve over the cauliflower and, if liked, sprinkle with a little finely chopped parsley. Serve hot.

BUTTERED CUCUMBERS

FRANCE

Serves: 4

2 large green cucumbers
60 g (2 oz) butter
salt and white pepper
1 tablespoon chopped chives

Peel the cucumbers, cut in halves lengthways and scoop out the seeds. Cut the cucumber halves in half again crossways and each piece into four or five strips. Melt the butter in wok over low heat, add the cucumber and cook, turning the pieces frequently, until they are coated with butter. Season with salt and pepper. Cover and cook on low heat for 4 or 5 minutes. They should be tender but not too soft. Serve at once, sprinkled with chives.

BRAISED FENNEL AND ONIONS

ITALY

Serves: 6

3 or 4 large bulbs fennel
2 medium onions
2 tablespoons butter or olive oil
salt and pepper
3 tablespoons stock or water

Slice fennel and onions into rings. Heat butter or oil in wok over low heat and toss the sliced vegetables in it for 2 minutes. Season with salt and pepper, add the liquid, cover and cook on very low heat for 15 minutes or until both fennel and onions are soft and transparent, adding a little more liquid if required. Serve hot.

RICE AND NOODLES

CHICKEN AND PORK FRIED RICE

BURMA

Serves: 6-8

See picture page 94

2 cups short grain rice
1 pair Chinese sausages
3 tablespoons peanut oil
3 eggs, beaten
1 teaspoon finely chopped garlic
1–2 teaspoons shrimp paste
1 red capsicum, finely diced
4 spring onions, finely chopped
1 cup small cooked prawns
½ cup cooked pork, diced
1 cup cooked chicken breasts, boned
   and diced
2 tablespoons dark soy
2 tablespoons water
2 teaspoons chilli sauce
1 teaspoon sesame oil

Garnish:
½ cup coriander leaves
omelette strips (see method)

Put 3½ cups water in a saucepan, add rice and Chinese sausages and bring to the boil. Cover with well-fitting lid, turn heat to low and cook for 20 minutes without lifting the lid. When cooked, turn rice on to tray and leave to cool. Separate sausages, slice thin diagonally and set aside. Grease wok lightly and make 3 omelettes with beaten eggs, cut into strips and set aside.

Heat remaining oil in wok, add garlic, shrimp paste, capsicum, half the spring onions and stir fry for 1 minute. Add cooked rice to wok and stir fry till warmed through. Add prawns, pork, chicken and sausage, and stir till heated through. In a bowl mix together soy, water, chilli sauce and sesame oil, and pour over rice in the wok. Raise heat, add remaining spring onions and half the omelette strips, stir and blend well. Serve hot, garnished with chopped coriander leaves and remaining omelette strips.

CRAB AND PORK FRIED RICE

KOREA

Serves: 4

2 tablespoons peanut oil
1 clove garlic, crushed
1 teaspoon finely grated fresh ginger
½ cup flaked cooked crab meat
½-1 cup chopped cooked pork
4 cups cooked rice
½ cup finely sliced spring onions
1 teaspoon salt or to taste

Heat oil in a wok and fry garlic, ginger, crab and pork together, stirring. Add rice and continue to stir and toss until rice is fried. Add spring onions and sprinkle salt over. Toss to mix thoroughly, taste for seasoning. Serve hot.

STIR-FRIED FRESH NOODLES

SINGAPORE

Serves: 4-6

500 g (1 lb) fresh wheat noodles (Hokkien mee)
4 rashers bacon
250 g (8 oz) lean steak
250 g (8 oz) small prawns
3 tablespoons oil
3 teaspoons chilli bean sauce
1 teaspoon finely chopped garlic
1 teaspoon finely chopped fresh ginger
2 cups shredded white Chinese cabbage
4 spring onions, cut into 5 cm (2 inch) lengths
¾ cup hot water
2 tablespoons light soy sauce

Put noodles in colander and steam over boiling water for 5 minutes. Meanwhile, remove rind and cut bacon into fine strips. Cut steak into paper-thin slices and then into shreds. Shell and de-vein prawns. Heat wok, add the oil and when hot fry the bacon for 1 minute. Add the beef, prawns, chilli bean sauce, garlic and ginger and stir fry until beef changes colour. Add cabbage and spring onions and stir fry 1 minute, then add noodles, hot water and soy sauce.

Cover and simmer on very low heat for 5-8 minutes, uncovering and turning noodles over every few minutes so they do not stick on bottom of wok. When noodles have absorbed all liquid and are soft (but not mushy) the dish is ready. Serve hot.

STIR-FRIED RICE NOODLES   MALAYSIA

Serves: 6

1 kg (2 lb) kway teow (fresh rice
  noodles)
250 g (8 oz) chicken breast, boned
250 g (8 oz) small raw prawns
125 g (4 oz) barbecued pork
2 lap cheong (Chinese sausage)
1 cup fresh bean sprouts
4 tablespoons lard or oil
1 teaspoon finely chopped garlic
2 medium onions, sliced
4 fresh red chillies, seeded and
  chopped
2 tablespoons dark soy sauce
1 tablespoon light soy sauce
1 tablespoon oyster sauce
3 eggs, beaten
salt and pepper to taste

Garnish:
5 spring onions, chopped

Cut kway teow into 6 mm (¼ inch) strips. Put into a large bowl, cover
with hot water and soak until strips separate easily, then drain in colander.
Cut chicken breast into bite-size pieces. Shell and de-vein prawns. Cut
barbecued pork into thin slices. Steam the lap cheong and cut into very thin
slices. Pinch any straggly 'tails' off bean sprouts.

Heat 2 tablespoons of the lard or oil in a wok and fry the garlic, onions
and chillies over medium heat, stirring, until they are soft. Add chicken,
prawns, pork and lap cheong and stir fry for 2–3 minutes or until cooked.
Add bean sprouts and toss once or twice, then remove mixture from wok.
Heat remaining lard or oil, and when very hot add the kway teow and stir
fry until it is heated through. Add all the seasonings and toss well to mix.
Push kway teow to sides of wok, pour beaten egg into the centre and stir
constantly until it is set. Mix egg with kway teow and return fried mixture
to wok, toss to mix well and serve hot, garnished with spring onions.

Note: Fresh rice noodles are sold at Chinese grocery stores as 'sa hor fun'
and some are already cut in strips.

SAVOURY FRIED RICE   MALAYSIA

Serves: 4

2½ tablespoons ghee or oil
3 large leeks, finely sliced or 12
  spring onions, chopped
1 medium onion, finely sliced
2 or 3 fresh chillies, seeded and
  sliced
250 g (8 oz) ham or bacon, chopped
6 eggs
1 teaspoon salt
½ teaspoon freshly ground black
  pepper
4 cups cold cooked rice
2 tablespoons light soy sauce

In a large wok heat ghee and fry leeks, onion, chillies and ham until leeks
and onion are golden. Beat eggs with salt and pepper, pour into pan and stir
over medium heat until eggs are creamy and almost set. Add rice and mix
thoroughly. Cook, stirring and tossing, until heated through. Sprinkle
with soy sauce, mixing well. Serve as a light meal, by itself or
accompanied by pickles or chutneys.

FRIED RICE WITH PORK AND WATER CHESTNUTS

CHINA

Serves: 4-5

250 g (8 oz) cooked pork
1 small can water chestnuts
4 tablespoons peanut oil
1 teaspoon sesame oil
1 teaspoon crushed garlic
1 teaspoon finely grated fresh ginger
4 cups cold cooked rice
2 tablespoons soy sauce
2 eggs, beaten
salt and pepper to taste
½ cup finely sliced spring onions

Cut the pork into small dice. Chop the water chestnuts. Heat peanut oil and sesame oil in wok until medium heat is reached, add the garlic and ginger and stir over low heat for a few seconds. Do not let them brown. Add the rice and fry over high heat, stirring and tossing constantly, until all the rice is heated through and starting to colour. Sprinkle the soy sauce over and continue mixing.

Add pork and water chestnuts and stir well, then move rice to sides of wok, leaving a space in the centre. Season the eggs with salt and pepper, pour into wok and cook, stirring the eggs, until they are almost dry. Now mix through the rice. Add the spring onions and continue to fry and mix for a further minute or two. Serve hot.

NASI GORENG

INDONESIA

Serves: 4-6

peanut oil for frying
3 tablespoons dried onion flakes
salt and pepper to taste
2 medium onions
1 teaspoon finely chopped garlic
½ teaspoon trasi or blachan (dried
    shrimp paste)
250 g (8 oz) raw prawns, shelled and
    de-veined
500 g (1 lb) lean steak, cut into fine
    strips
6 spring onions, chopped
4 cups cold boiled rice
2 tablespoons dark soy sauce

Garnish:
1 green cucumber, thinly sliced
omelette strips (see method)
fried onion flakes (see method)

Heat wok, add 2 tablespoons oil and fry dried onion flakes, on low heat, for a few seconds only. When brown, remove from heat at once as they burn easily. Set aside. Beat eggs with salt and pepper to taste. In the same oil used for frying the onion flakes, make a flat omelette with half the beaten eggs. Turn on to a plate to cool. Repeat process with remaining beaten eggs. When cool, place one omelette on top of the other, roll up and cut into thin strips.

Chop onions roughly and place in blender container with garlic and trasi. Cover and blend to a paste. (If electric blender is not available, finely chop onions and garlic and dissolve trasi in a little hot water.) Combine these ingredients.

Heat 3 tablespoons of oil in a wok and fry the blended ingredients, stirring constantly, until cooked. Add prawns and meat to wok and stir-fry until they are cooked. Add remaining 2 tablespoons of oil and when hot stir in the spring onions and rice, mixing thoroughly and frying until it is heated through. Sprinkle with soy sauce and mix evenly.

Serve the fried rice garnished with strips of omelette, fried onion flakes and very thin slices of cucumber.

FRIED RICE WITH MIXED VEGETABLES

CHINA

Serves: 6

See picture page 111

500 g (1 lb) short grain rice
3 cups water
12 dried Chinese mushrooms
1 or 2 large leeks
4 stalks celery
250 g (8 oz) green beans
125 g (4 oz) fresh bean sprouts
2 medium carrots
1 piece canned bamboo shoot
3 tablespoons peanut oil
1 tablespoon sesame oil
1 teaspoon finely grated fresh ginger
1 teaspoon finely grated garlic
1 cup finely sliced spring onions
½ cup mushroom liquid
2 tablespoons light soy sauce
salt to taste

Put rice and water into a heavy saucepan with a close fitting lid, bring to the boil over high heat, then turn heat very low, cover pan tightly and cook for 20 minutes. Turn out of pan, spread on large tray or baking dish and allow to cool. Refrigerate. This should be done some hours before rice is to be fried, or even the day before.

Soak mushrooms in hot water for 30 minutes, then squeeze out as much liquid as possible and reserve liquid. With a sharp knife cut off and discard stems. Cut mushroom caps into thin slices and if they are large mushrooms cut the slices across so that slices are not too long.

Wash leeks well in cold water, making sure all the grit between the leaves is washed away. Cut into thin slices, using all the white portion and about 5-7 cm (2-3 inches) of the green leaves. String celery and green beans and cut into very thin diagonal slices. Wash and drain bean sprouts and pinch off any straggly brown 'tails'. Grate carrots coarsely and cut bamboo shoot into matchstick strips.

Heat peanut oil and sesame oil in a large wok, add ginger and garlic and fry over medium low heat, stirring well, for 30 seconds. Add mushrooms, leeks, celery, beans and carrots and stir fry over high heat for 3 minutes. Add bean sprouts and bamboo shoots and fry 1 minute longer.

Add rice, toss and fry over high heat until all the grains are heated through. Add spring onions. Mix mushroom liquid and soy sauce together and sprinkle evenly over rice. Continue stirring to mix well together and season to taste with salt. Serve hot.

CHILLI FRIED RICE

THAILAND

Serves: 4

185 g (6 oz) canned crab meat
3 tablespoons peanut oil
2 medium onions, finely chopped
2 fresh red or green chillies, seeded
 and sliced
2 teaspoons finely chopped garlic
1 pork chop, finely diced
500 g (1 lb) raw prawns, shelled and
 de-veined
4 cups cooked rice
3 eggs, beaten
salt and pepper to taste
3 tablespoons fish sauce
1 tablespoon chilli sauce
¾ cup chopped spring onions,
 including green tops
¾ cup chopped fresh coriander leaves

Garnish:
chilli flowers

Flake the crab meat and remove any bony tinnue, set aside. Heat wok, add oil and fry onions, sliced chillies and garlic until soft. Add diced pork and stir fry until cooked, then add prawns (chopped into smaller pieces if they are large). Stir fry for 2 minutes until prawns turn pink. Add crab meat to wok and stir well with the pork and prawns.

Add rice to wok and toss thoroughly until mixed and heated through. Push rice to side of wok and pour the beaten eggs, seasoned with salt and pepper, into the centre. Scramble eggs until they set, then mix through the rice. Sprinkle fish sauce and chilli sauce over rice, raise heat, stir well for 1 minute, then remove from heat. Add the spring onions and coriander leaves and mix through the rice. Garnish with chilli flowers and serve.

STIR-FRIED CHICKEN WITH RICE VERMICELLI

SINGAPORE

Serves : 4

250 g (8 oz) rice vermicelli
 (mehoon)
500 g (1 lb) chicken breasts
4 tablespoons peanut oil
1 cup cubed raw potato
2 medium onions, finely sliced
2 teaspoons finely chopped garlic
2 tablespoons light soy sauce
½ cup water
¼ teaspoon ground black pepper
3 teaspoons sugar
1 tablespoon chilli sauce
salt to taste

Put the rice vermicelli in a large bowl, pour warm water over and leave to soak for 5 minutes, then drain in a colander and set aside. Remove skin and bone from chicken breasts and cut meat into bite-size pieces. Heat wok, add oil and when oil starts to smoke, add the cubed potato and stir fry over high heat for 2 minutes, then reduce heat to medium and continue frying until cubes are golden. Remove with slotted spoon and set aside.

Add the onions and garlic and fry 2 minutes, stirring, on medium low heat, then add the chicken, stir fry for 5 minutes or until chicken is cooked. Add the drained rice vermicelli and half the soy sauce and water mixed together. Toss and stir until water is absorbed, then add remaining soy sauce and water. Add pepper, sugar, chilli sauce and continue stirring until liquid is almost all absorbed. Stir in potatoes, adjust seasoning, and heat through. Serve immediately.

COMBINATION FRIED NOODLES

PHILIPPINES

Serves: 6-8

500 g (1 lb) cooked prawns
500 g (1 lb) thin egg noodles
4 tablespoons lard and oil,
 equal quantities
3 teaspoons finely chopped garlic
3 medium onions, finely sliced
1 cup diced cooked chicken
1 cup cooked pork, cut in thin strips
¾ cup ham, cut in thin strips
1 cup shredded Chinese cabbage
3 tablespoons light soy sauce
1 cup hot stock or water
salt and pepper to taste

Garnish:
lemon wedges

Shell and de-vein prawns and cut into pieces if large. Soak noodles in warm water while bringing a large pan of water to the boil. Drain noodles and drop them into the fast boiling water, bring back to the boil and cook for 2 minutes. Do not overcook. Drain immediately, spread on a large baking tray lined with kitchen paper and allow to dry for at least 30 minutes, sprinkling a little oil over to prevent sticking together.

Heat wok, add 1 tablespoon of lard/oil mixture and when very hot fry noodles, a handful at a time, until golden on both sides, adding more lard to the wok as necessary. Remove noodles from wok. Heat a little more lard and fry separately the garlic, onion, prawns, chicken, pork and ham. Set aside some of each for garnishing the dish and return the rest to the wok together with cabbage, soy sauce, 1 cup hot stock or water, salt and pepper. Cook uncovered until almost dry, then return noodles and heat through, stirring and tossing well to mix. Arrange on serving platter and garnish with the reserved ingredients and wedges of lemon.

TABLE-TOP COOKING

VIETNAMESE SOUP

VIETNAM

Serves: 6-8

This is a meal in one dish that is particularly suitable for table-top cooking. The combination of crisp, half-cooked vegetables and tender slices of beef in a well-flavoured stock is delicious, as well as being low in calories. Keep the stock simmering in an electric wok or one heated by a portable gas ring. Have all the other ingredients arranged on separate serving dishes, and assemble the meal in individual bowls.

Stock:
3 kg (6 lb) beef rib bones
500 g (1 lb) gravy beef
2 onions, sliced
thumb-size piece of fresh ginger root
stick of cinnamon
1 teaspoon whole black peppercorns
salt to taste

First make the stock. Put bones and gravy beef in a large pan, add cold water to cover and the sliced onions, scraped and sliced ginger, cinnamon stick, whole peppercorns. Bring to the boil, turn heat very low, cover and simmer for at least six hours. Add salt to taste.

If using fresh rice noodles (sa ho fun, look fun, chee cheong fun), slice them into 1 cm (½ inch) strips and pour boiling hot water over, leave for 15 minutes, then drain. Or steam in a colander for 5 minutes. If using dried rice noodles, they have to be soaked in warm water for at least 2 hours, then drained and cooked in boiling water until just tender. Drain well.

For serving at table:
500 g (1 lb) fresh rice noodles
** or 250 g (8 oz) dried rice noodles**
500 g (1 lb) fresh bean sprouts
6 spring onions
4 firm ripe tomatoes
2 white onions
500 g (1 lb) rump steak
fish sauce
lemon wedges
fresh red or green chillies, chopped
chopped fresh coriander leaves

Prepare other ingredients. Scald bean sprouts by pouring boiling water over them in a colander. Run cold water over. If necessary, pinch off any straggly brown 'tails'. Slice spring onions thinly. Cut tomatoes in half lengthways, then slice each half. Peel and slice onions thinly. Slice steak paper-thin in bite-size pieces. Arrange on serving plates.

To serve: Have the strained stock simmering in wok at the table. Put a large soup bowl before each guest and in each bowl put a spoonful of noodles and another of bean sprouts. With chopsticks, put a few slices of beef, tomato and onion in a large ladle and immerse in the boiling stock until beef begins to lose its redness. Do not overcook — beef should be pale pink. Pour contents of the ladle over noodles and bean sprouts.

Each guest adds fish sauce, lemon juice, chillies and fresh coriander to taste.

BANQUET FIREPOT

Serves: 6

500 g (1 lb) barbecued pork
8 dried Chinese mushrooms
2 tablespoons light soy sauce
1 tablespoon sugar
500 g (1 lb) fresh prawns
500 g (1 lb) minced pork
1 teaspoon finely grated fresh ginger
3 spring onions, finely chopped
1 clove garlic, crushed
1 teaspoon salt
1 tablespoon cornflour
1 tablespoon cold water
1 canned bamboo shoot
12 water chestnuts
3 cups shredded Chinese cabbage
10 cups strong beef stock
omelettes made with 2 eggs, cut in
   thin streds

Dipping Sauce:
½ cup light soy sauce
½ cup dry sherry
1 teaspoon fresh ginger juice

This is a variation on the Steamboat, Firekettle or Mongolian Firepot, which is a utensil with a chimney surrounded by a moat which holds the food and simmering stock. The original steamboat is heated with live coals placed in the chimney, but an electric wok or a wok placed on a portable table cooker may successfully be used instead. The meal is one which combines nourishment with entertainment as guests cook their own choice of food at the table. Set a rice bowl and sauce bowl at each place, also wooden chopsticks and small wire baskets for cooking the food in the stock and retrieving small items.

Slice barbecued pork thinly. Soak mushrooms 30 minutes in hot water, discard stems, put mushrooms into a saucepan with a cup of the water they were soaked in, add soy sauce, sugar, cover and simmer until liquid is almost completely evaporated. Shell, de-vein prawns, leaving tails on. Combine minced pork with ginger, spring onions, garlic, salt and cornflour mixed with water. Form into balls about the size of a large marble and simmer in water for 10 minutes. Remove and set aside. Drain bamboo shoot and cut into fancy shapes. Cut water chestnuts in round slices. Combine sauce ingredients and divide between individual sauce bowls.

Put shredded Chinese cabbage in the wok, and arrange the different items attractively in sections on the cabbage. Take to the table. Bring the stock to boiling point and pour gently into the wok, disturbing the arrangement as little as possible. Add only enough stock to come to the level of the food and reserve the rest for adding to the wok later.

Heat until stock simmers and cover with lid for 5 minutes or until all the food is heated through, in which time prawns should be cooked. If prawns are large, allow more time. Adjust heat so that it keeps simmering.

Each person takes a piece of food from the wok, dips it in his individual bowl of sauce and eats it with hot white rice. When all the food has been eaten, add remaining stock and bring to the boil, add a dash of Chinese wine or dry sherry and serve as a soup to finish the meal.

Note: If preferred, raw foods such as very thinly sliced beef, chicken, fish, vegetables, bean curd and so on, may be arranged on platters and guests may cook their own choice, holding the pieces in the boiling stock until cooked to their liking.

SHABU-SHABU

Serves: 6-8

This is the Japanese of Mongolian 'fire pot' or Singapore 'steamboat'. Guests cook their own meal at the table, holding pieces of steak and vegetables with chopsticks and dipping them into simmering stock. The name of the dish is meant to convey the gentle swishing sound made as the food is cooked.

1 kg (2 lb) fillet steak
1 small white Chinese cabbage
  (hakusai)
12 spring onions
2 tender carrots
500 g (1 lb) button mushrooms
8-10 cups chicken stock

Sesame Seed Sauce:
4 tablespoons sesame seeds
2 tablespoons mild white vinegar or
  lemon juice
¾ cup Japanese soy sauce
3 tablespoons finely chopped spring
  onion
2 teaspoons finely grated fresh
  ginger

Partially freeze the meat, just enough to make it firm so it can be sliced very thinly.

Cut cabbage into short lengths. Cut spring onions into bite-size lengths. Cut carrots in round slices, parboil and drain. Wipe mushrooms with damp kitchen paper, trim ends of stalks and cut in halves. Arrange food on large serving platter, cover and refrigerate.

At serving time pour stock into electric wok or wok over portable gas burner. Heat and place in the centre of table, taking care to adequately protect table from heat. Keep stock simmering throughout the meal, adding more as necessary.

Set each place with a bowl, chopsticks and individual bowl for dipping sauce. Also serve a bowl of hot white rice so guests can help themselves. Ingredients are picked up with chopsticks and held in the simmering stock until just done, then transferred to individual bowls, dipped in sauce and eaten with rice. Care should be taken not to overcook meat and vegetables. Steak should be pale pink when cooked and vegetables tender but still crisp.

When all the meat and vegetables have been eaten, the stock is served as a soup, bowls being lifted to the lips, Japanese fashion.

Sesame Seed Sauce: Lightly brown sesame seeds in a dry pan over moderate heat, stirring constantly with a spoon or shaking pan. When seeds are golden brown turn on to a plate to cool, then crush in mortar and pestle. Combine with remaining ingredients. Alternatively, put ingredients in electric blender and blend on high speed for a few seconds.

TEMPURA

Serves: 4

16 medium-size raw prawns
500 g (1 lb) fillets of fish
1 canned lotus root
1 can baby corn cobs
3 canned winter bamboo shoots
thinly sliced sweet potato
thinly sliced eggplant
thinly sliced carrots or green beans
whole snow peas, strings removed
spring onions, cut into short lengths

Tempura Batter:
1 egg
1 cup ice-cold water
pinch bicarbonate of soda
¾ cup tempura flour or unsifted plain
   flour

For Frying:
3 cups vegetable oil
½ cup sesame oil

For Serving:
4 tablespoons grated white radish
   (daikon)
2 tablespoons finely grated fresh
   ginger

Tempura Sauce:
3 tablespoons mirin or dry sherry
3 tablespoons Japanese soy sauce
1 cup dashi (made from packet)
pinch salt
pinch monosodium glutamate,
   optional

For a leisurely meal cooked at the table, it would be hard to find anything more acceptable than tempura. The deep fried seafood and vegetables are coated with a very thin, crisp butter so that the food steams within the coating and is never heavy or greasy. The secret is not to add too many pieces at a time to the oil, thus lowering the temperature too much. An electric wok or one placed over a portable gas ring is ideal for cooking tempura, as the shape means you require less oil. Use vegetables as available.

Shell prawns, leaving tails on. Remove the vein, wash and dry well on kitchen paper. Slice fish fillets into thin, bite-size slices, first removing any skin and bones. Drain all the canned vegetables thoroughly and dry them on kitchen paper. Cut lotus root crossways into thin slices. Slice bamboo shoots and if large cut to suitable size. Arrange ingredients attractively on a tray, cover and refrigerate until required.

Tempura Sauce: Heat mirin in a small saucepan, remove from heat and ignite with a match. Shake pan gently until flame dies, add all other ingredients and bring to a boil. Cool to room temperature, taste and adjust seasoning if necessary.

Set before each place a plate lined with a paper napkin, a small bowl for dipping sauce and another small bowl with a tablespoon of grated white radish and 2 teaspoons of grated fresh ginger. Prepare sauce by mixing together the ingredients.

Tempura Batter: Break egg into bowl containing iced water and beat until frothy. Add bicarbonate of soda and flour and beat just until flour is mixed in. Do not overbeat. Batter should be thin. If it seems too thick, add a few drops of iced water. Keep batter cold throughout cooking.

No more than 10 minutes before serving, make batter and stand the bowl in a larger bowl containing ice. Heat both oils to 190°C (375°F). If sesame oil is not available it may be omitted, but it gives a distinctive flavour to the food.

When guests are seated, dip pieces of food one at a time into the batter and drop into the oil. Do not fry more than about 6 pieces at a time, as the temperature of the oil must be kept moderately high for best results. As each piece turns golden (this should take only a minute or very little longer) lift it from the oil with a perforated spoon, drain for a few seconds on absorbent paper, then serve immediately to guests, who dip each piece in the sauce and eat it while crisp and hot. The radish and ginger are mixed into the sauce to suit individual taste.

Note: Ready-to-use tempura sauce may be purchased in bottles if preferred.

SUKIYAKI

JAPAN

Serves: 4-6

750 g (1½ lb) tender steak in one
    piece
12 spring onions
1 cup sliced bamboo shoots
250 g (8 oz) fresh mushrooms, sliced
2 medium onions
250 g (8 oz) fresh bean sprouts
6 leaves white Chinese cabbage
    (hakusai)
1 packet shirataki or 60 g (2 oz)
    cellophane noodles
6 pieces tofu (bean curd), optional
piece of beef suet or little oil
Japanese soy sauce
sugar, sake or dry sherry, beef stock

This famous Japanese dish is usually cooked on a heavy griddle or teppan, but may also be cooked in a wok. Have all the ingredients arranged on a serving tray and cook a third at a time, cooking the next batch when the first has been eaten. Ideal for table-top cooking.

Japanese prefer well-marbled steak to very lean types, so choose Scotch fillet or other suitable cut. Freeze the steak for an hour or until just firm enough to cut in very thin slices. Wash and trim spring onions and cut into bite-size lengths, using tender part of the green portion as well as the white. Use winter bamboo shoots if possible as they are more tender. Slice thinly and cut into bite-size pieces. Wipe mushrooms over with damp kitchen paper and slice thickly or cut into quarters.

Peel onions, cut in quarter lengthways, then across into eighths. Separate layers. Wash bean sprouts and pinch off any straggly 'tails'. Wash Chinese cabbage and cut into bite-size pieces, discarding tough portions of leaves.

Cook the noodles in boiling water for 10 minutes, drain and cut into short lengths. Arrange ingredients on a tray and have ready before starting to cook.

Heat wok and rub over with beef suet until well-greased. Or heat a tablespoon of oil and swirl pan to coat. Add one third of each vegetable to wok and fry on high heat for a minute or two. Push to side of wok and add a third of the beef in one layer. When cooked on one side (this should take only a minute because meat is so thinly sliced) turn and cook other side. Sprinkle with Japanese soy sauce, sugar and sake to taste, add a little stock to moisten all the meat and vegetables. Mix in a third of the noodles and tofu and heat through. Serve immediately, each person helping himself from the pan.

As each batch is cooked, turn off heat. When it has all been eaten, wipe out pan with paper towels, heat suet or oil and start to cook the next batch.

Traditionally, each diner breaks an egg into his bowl and beats it lightly with chopsticks, then dips the hot food in beaten egg before eating, but some prefer to omit this step. Serve hot white rice with sukiyaki.

Sukiyaki may be cooked in a wok placed on a portable gas ring at the table or for outdoor meals, or in an electric wok.

Opposite: Fried Rice with Mixed Vegetables, recipe page 103.

110

SWEETS
AND DESSERTS

Some of these sweets are deep fried, which makes them a natural for wok cooking as the shape of the wok means less oil is used. Others are steamed, also using the wok to advantage.

Then there are those which are easily recognisable as chafing dish desserts. If you have a chafing dish, well and good. But if you haven't, that needn't stop you, now that you have a wok. With an electric wok or one used on a table-top gas burner, you can prepare these desserts right at the table. Or assemble them, even cook them beforehand and reheat them for your guests so they may be served piping hot. If you prefer to perform in the kitchen you can do that too, and bring them flaming to the table for a touch of drama.

Opposite: Savarin with Strawberries, recipe page 114.

SAVARIN WITH STRAWBERRIES

FRANCE

Serves: 6

See picture page 112

This rich yeast cake is usually baked, but I have found it steams to a delicate, light texture and may be reheated by steaming again, briefly, if made ahead and frozen.

½ cup milk
15 g (½ oz) fresh yeast
1 tablespoon sugar
2 cups flour
2 eggs, beaten
125 g (4 oz) butter

Syrup:
1 cup sugar
1 cup water
¼ cup Grand Marnier or rum

For finishing the Savarin:
1 cup apricot jam for glazing
2 punnets strawberries
300 ml thickened cream
1 tablespoon caster sugar
½ teaspoon vanilla essence

Heat the milk in a small saucepan until bubbles form around edge, then allow to cool to lukewarm. Crumble yeast over the milk, add sugar and dissolve. Sift flour into a large bowl, make a well in the centre and pour in the yeast mixture. Sprinkle some of the flour over the liquid, cover with a clean tea towel and leave in a warm place for 10-15 minutes until yeast mixture starts to froth.

Add the beaten eggs and beat until smooth, then add the butter softened at room temperature and mix well until thoroughly incorporated. Cover with tea towel and leave in a warm, draught-free place until it doubles in volume, about 45 minutes. Punch down and knead firmly to expel air bubbles. Put mixture into a buttered savarin mould and allow to prove in a warm place until dough rises again, 35-45 minutes.

Place mould in a bamboo steamer and steam in a wok over gently boiling water for about 35 minutes or until risen and firm to the touch and a fine skewer inserted in the centre comes out clean. Remove from heat and pour syrup over. Leave for 20 minutes or until syrup has been absorbed.

Syrup: Put sugar and water into a small heavy saucepan and heat until sugar dissolves, then boil fast for about 5 minutes. Remove from heat and stir in liqueur.

Turn out on a serving plate. Heat apricot jam until liquid, strain through a sieve, then glaze the savarin with the jam. Leave for a few minutes to allow the glaze to set, then fill centre of savarin with strawberries and arrange more berries around.

Serve warm, with a bowl of chilled cream which has been whipped and flavoured with icing sugar and vanilla.

Note: If liked, the strawberries may be macerated in liqueur and caster sugar.

Important. The woven lids are ideal for steaming bread and cake mixtures as moisture does not collect on the underside, as happens with metal lids. If a bamboo steamer with woven lid is not available, the savarin may be steamed on a metal tray and covered with a metal lid but in this case place a piece of foil lightly over the savarin mould to prevent moisture from dripping on to top of savarin.

CRULLERS

2 eggs
⅓ cup caster sugar
finely grated rind of 1 lemon
½ teaspoon vanilla
2 tablespoons melted butter
2 tablespoons milk
1¾ cups sifted flour
½ teaspoon baking powder
pinch salt
oil for deep frying
icing sugar for dusting

Beat the eggs until frothy, add the sugar gradually and continue beating until thick and light. Add the lemon rind, vanilla, butter and milk and mix well. Sift together the dry ingredients, add to first mixture and mix to form a soft dough. Roll out on a lightly floured board to a thickness of ¼ inch. If necessary, wrap dough in plastic and chill slightly first. Cut with a pastry wheel or sharp knife into finger-size strips. Heat oil for deep frying and fry strips, a few at a time, until puffed and golden. Drain on absorbent paper and serve sprinkled with icing sugar.

CENCI

Thin strips of pastry, tied in loose knots and deep fried, are sprinkled with icing sugar just before serving.

1 cup plain flour
1 egg
1 egg yolk
3 teaspoons port wine or rum
2 teaspoons icing sugar
oil for deep frying
extra icing sugar

Sift the flour into a bowl. Beat together the egg, egg yolk, rum and icing sugar. Pour into the bowl and mix to a dough. Knead on a lightly floured board for 10 minutes or until the dough is smooth and elastic. Wrap in greaseproof paper or plastic and chill for about 1 hour.

Roll out half the pastry on a floured board until paper thin. Cut into narrow strips about 15 cm (6 inches) long. Tie each strip loosely in a knot. Heat about 2 cups oil in a wok and when very hot fry the pastry knots, 3 or 4 at a time, until they are golden brown. Remove from wok with slotted spoon and drain on absorbent paper. Repeat with remaining dough. Sift icing sugar over before serving.

CRÈME CARAMEL

FRANCE

Serves: 4

4 tablespoons sugar
¼ cup water
2 eggs
1 egg yolk
¼ cup caster sugar
¾ cup milk
½ cup cream
1 teaspoon vanilla

Put sugar and water into a small saucepan over medium heat and cook without stirring until the sugar melts and eventually the syrup turns golden brown. Pour into 4 individual ramekins or custard cups and rotate the cups to coat base and sides with caramel.

Beat the eggs and egg yolk with the caster sugar until well mixed, add the milk and cream and mix well. Stir in the vanilla. Strain into a jug, then pour into the prepared cups. Put water into wok to come just under steaming rack and bring to the boil. Turn heat low so water just simmers, place custard cups on rack and cover loosely with foil, then place cover on wok and steam over simmering water for 30 minutes. Test by inserting a knife in the centre of one of the cups. It should come out clean when custards are done. Remove from heat, cool and chill. Run a knife around edge of each cup and turn out on dessert plates. Serve chilled.

SWEET WONTONS

CHINA

Makes about 50

250 g (8 oz) pitted dates
¼ cup coarsely chopped walnuts
1 teaspoon finely grated orange or
    lemon rind
1 tablespoon orange juice
250 g (8 oz) wonton wrappers
oil for deep frying
icing sugar

These crisp little pastries store well in an airtight container, but are nicest served fairly soon after they are made. The filling may be dates and walnuts, or one of the canned sweet pastes made from lotus nuts or red beans which are sold in Chinese stores. The wonton wrappers may also be purchased from Chinese grocery stores.

Chop dates finely, mix with the walnuts, grated rind and just enough juice to moisten to a moulding consistency. Form into small rolls as thick as a pencil and about an inch and a half long. Put a roll of date mixture diagonally on each square of wonton pastry, place corner of pastry over and roll up, completely enclosing filling. Twist ends of the pastry, putting a finger in the end so it is shaped like a miniature Christmas cracker.

When they are all made, heat oil in wok and fry a few at a time in very hot oil, turning them until they are golden brown on all sides. This does not take long as the pastry is so fine and they should be done in about 2 minutes. Lift out each batch as it is fried and drain on absorbent paper.

Serve the wontons slightly warm or allow them to cool. Arrange on a serving plate and sprinkle a light dusting of icing sugar over, using a fine sieve.

PINEAPPLE AND RAISIN FLAMBÉ

JAMAICA

Serves: 4

¼ cup seedless raisins
¼ cup brandy
1 small, ripe pineapple
  or small can pineapple pieces
60 g (2 oz) butter
4 tablespoons sugar
½ teaspoon ground allspice
¾ cup orange or pineapple juice
extra 3 tablespoons brandy or rum
whipped cream or ice cream

Soak raisins in brandy for 20 minutes. Peel pineapple, cut in wedges lengthways and remove core, then cut fruit into bite-size pieces. Heat butter in wok and fry the pineapple and raisins until heated through. Add sugar, spice and fruit juice and simmer for 5 minutes or until liquid is syrupy. Transfer to serving dish, heat extra rum or brandy, pour over fruits and ignite. Serve hot with whipped cream or ice cream.

BANANAS CALYPSO

WEST INDIES

Serves: 4

4 large firm bananas
60 g (2 oz) butter
3 tablespoons brown sugar
½ cup dark rum
1 tablespoon Angostura bitters
½ cup toasted slivered almonds
vanilla ice cream

Peel bananas and cut in halves crossways. Heat butter in wok on low heat and when melted add the bananas and fry until golden all over, turning bananas carefully. Add sugar, half the rum and the Angostura bitters and when the sugar dissolves, transfer to a serving dish. Scatter the toasted almonds over. Heat remaining rum with 1 teaspoon sugar, ignite and pour, flaming, over the fruit. Serve hot, accompanied by vanilla ice cream.

FLAMBÉED FRUITS   FRANCE

Serves: 6

1 large can peach or apricot halves
2 or 3 tablespoons peach or apricot
   liqueur
2 teaspoons arrowroot or cornflour
8-10 almond macaroons or amoretti
   biscuits
¼ cup brandy

Drain canned fruit, reserving syrup. Put the fruit into a bowl and sprinkle with the liqueur. Cover and set aside. Mix arrowroot or cornflour smoothly with a little of the syrup, heat remaining syrup in wok until simmering. On low heat, stir in the arrowroot and stir constantly until thick and clear. Add fruit and spoon sauce over until fruit is hot. Crumble the macaroons and put into serving dish. Arrange the fruits over the macaroons, heat brandy, ignite and pour over the fruits. Serve flaming. Pouring cream may accompany the fruits if liked.

RICE CALAS   NEW ORLEANS

Makes about 30 fritters

15 g (½ oz) fresh yeast
   or 2 teaspoons active dry yeast
½ cup warm water
1 cup cooked rice
2 eggs
⅓ cup sugar
½ cup plain flour
½ teaspoon salt (omit if rice is cooked
   with salt)
1 teaspoon freshly grated nutmeg
1 teaspoon vanilla essence
oil for deep frying
icing sugar for sprinkling

Sprinkle yeast over warm water in a bowl, leave to soften, then dissolve by stirring. Mash the rice with a fork and mix with the yeast. It does not matter if all the rice grains are not mashed — if rice is soft-boiled a light mashing is all that is needed. Cover and leave overnight.

Next day, beat eggs until frothy and add to rice mixture together with sugar. Sift the flour, salt and spice together and mix in, add vanilla and stir well.

Heat oil in a wok to a depth of at least 5 cm (2 inches) and when hot drop the mixture into the oil by teaspoonfuls. Do not cook too many at a time. Fry until golden brown, spooning the hot oil over and turning to cook both sides. Drain on absorbent paper. Serve warm, dusted with icing sugar.

BANANA NUT BREAD   JAMAICA

Makes 1 loaf

125 g (4 oz) butter
½ cup firmly packed brown sugar
1 teaspoon vanilla
1 egg
2½ cups plain flour
3½ teaspoons baking powder
¼ teaspoon salt
½ teaspoon freshly grated nutmeg
  or ground allspice
1½ cups very ripe mashed bananas
½ cup broken walnut kernels or raw
  cashews

Have butter softened at room temperature. Cream butter and sugar until light, add vanilla and egg and beat well. Sift together the flour, baking powder, salt and spice. Stir into creamed mixture alternately with the mashed bananas and fold in the nuts. Butter a large loaf pan and pour in the batter.

Pour about 3 cups water into wok and bring to the boil. Place steaming rack in wok, put loaf pan on the rack, cover with bamboo lid and steam over simmering water for 45-50 minutes or until a fine skewer inserted in centre of loaf comes out clean. After 30 minutes it will probably be necessary to add another cup or two of boiling water to the wok.

Let bread cool in the tin for a few minutes, then turn out on a wire cake cooler. Serve warm or cold.

Note: If bamboo lid is not available, cover loaf loosely with foil to prevent moisture from metal lid dripping on to surface.

DOUGH FOR STEAMED BUNS   CHINA

This dough is used with a variety of fillings, both savoury and sweet.

2½ cups plain flour
3½ teaspoons baking powder
3 tablespoons caster sugar
2 tablespoons softened lard
about ½ cup lukewarm water
½ teaspoon white vinegar
½ teaspoon salt

Sift flour and baking powder into a bowl, stir in sugar and rub in lard with fingertips until evenly distributed. Add water, vinegar and salt mixed together, and knead to a fairly soft dough. Shape into a smooth ball, cover and rest dough for 30 minutes.

YEAST DOUGH FOR STEAMED BUNS

CHINA

Makes about 16 buns

1¼ cups lukewarm water
15 g (½ oz) fresh yeast or
   2 teaspoons dry yeast
2 teaspoons sugar
4 cups plain flour
1 teaspoon salt
sesame oil

As an alternative to the baking powder dough, this yeast dough may be used for making Black Bean Buns or Pork Buns.

Measure ¼ cup water into a bowl, crumble fresh yeast over (or sprinkle dried yeast) and leave for 5 minutes to soften. Add sugar and stir to dissolve yeast and sugar, then add remaining warm water.

Sift flour and salt into another bowl, make a well in the middle and pour in the liquid. Sprinkle some of the flour over the top of the liquid and leave in a warm place for 10 minutes, by which time yeast should start to bubble and froth. Mix in the flour to form a soft dough and knead on a lightly floured board for 10-15 minutes or until dough is smooth and elastic. Form into a ball and put in a warm bowl lightly greased with sesame oil.

Cover and leave in a warm place until doubled in volume, then punch down the dough, knead lightly, cover and leave again until doubled in volume. Punch down, shape as required, leave to rise until almost double, then place rolls or buns on squares of greaseproof paper lightly rubbed with sesame oil, place in bamboo steamer, cover tightly and steam over gently boiling water for 8-10 minutes. These buns and rolls may be made soft and fresh by reheating over simmering water for 2 or 3 minutes.

Note: Do not uncover steamer as soon as rolls are cooked but turn off heat and leave for a few minutes. If uncovered immediately, the change of temperature will cause the top of buns to wrinkle. Peel off greaseproof paper on bottom of buns before serving.

BLACK BEAN BUNS CHINA

Makes 8

dough for steamed buns (see **pages 26 and 119**)
1 can sweet bean paste (dow saah)
squares of greaseproof paper
1 tablespoon sesame oil for brushing paper

Divide dough into 8 equal portions and roll each into a circle about 8 cm (3 inches) in diameter. Put a teaspoon of bean paste in the centre of each circle and mould and steam buns as described on page 26. Serve warm or at room temperature.

SWEET COCONUT BUNS CHINA

Makes 8

125 g (4 oz) slab sugar
¼ cup water
1 cup desiccated coconut
dough for steamed buns (see **pages 26 and 119**
1 tablespoon sesame oil for brushing

Put slab sugar and water into a small saucepan and heat gently until sugar is dissolved in the water, then stir in coconut and allow to cool. Mould and steam buns as described on page 26, using a teaspoonful of the coconut mixture for filling them.

GLOSSARY

ANNATTO SEEDS

Also called *achuete*, these are small red seeds used for colouring and flavouring Filipino food.

AROMATIC GINGER

See galangal, lesser.

BAGOONG

See shrimp paste.

BAMBOO SHOOT

Sold in cans, either water packed or braised. Unless otherwise stated, the recipes in this book use the water packed variety. After opening can, store in a bowl of fresh water in the refrigerator, changing water daily, for up to 10 days. Winter bamboo shoots are much smaller and more tender, and are called for in certain recipes; however, if they are not available, use the larger variety.

BEAN SPROUTS

Green *mung* beans are normally used for bean sprouts. They are sold fresh in most Chinese stores and in certain supermarkets and health food stores. The canned variety is not recommended. Substitute thinly sliced celery for a similar texture but different flavour. Fresh bean sprouts can be stored in a refrigerator for a week in a plastic bag; alternatively, cover with water and change water daily.

BESAN (CHICK PEA FLOUR)

Available at most stores selling Asian foods. Pea flour from health food stores can be substituted, but if it is coarse pass it through a fine sieve before using. Alternatively, roast yellow split peas in a heavy pan, stirring constantly and taking care not to burn them. Cool, then blend at high speed in an electric blender or pound with a mortar and pestle. Sift, then store the fine flour in an airtight container. *Besan* has a distinctive taste, and ordinary wheat flour cannot be substituted without loss of flavour.

BLACK BEANS, SALTED

Made from soy beans, heavily salted and sold in cans and jars. Rinse before using to avoid over salting recipes. Substitute extra soy sauce for flavour though not for appearance. Store in covered container in refrigerator after opening. It will keep for 6 months or longer. Add a little peanut oil if the top seems to dry out.

CANDLE NUT

A hard oily nut used to flavour and thicken Indonesian and Malaysian curries. The name arises because the nuts, when threaded on the mid-rib of a palm leaf, are used as a primitive candle. Use Brazil kernels as a substitute, though their flavour is sweeter than that of the candle nut.

CASHEW NUT (CASHEWS)

A sweet, kidney-shaped nut. In countries where the cashew tree is not grown, it is not possible to get the milky sweet fresh cashews. However, it is possible to buy raw cashews (as distinct from the roasted and salted cashews sold as snacks); nut shops, health food stores and grocers specialising in Asian ingredients stock the raw cashews.

CELLOPHANE NOODLES or BEAN THREAD VERMICELLI

Fine, transparent noodles made from the starch of green *mung* beans. May be soaked in hot water before use, or may require boiling according to the texture required. It is also deep fried straight from the packet, generally when used as a garnish or to provide a background for other foods.

CHILLI POWDER

Asian chilli powder is made from ground chillies. It is much hotter than the Mexican-style chilli powder, which is mostly ground cummin.

CHILLI SAUCE

There are two different types of chilli sauce. The Chinese style is made from chillies, salt and vinegar, and has a hot flavour. The Malaysian, Singaporean or Sri Lankan chilli sauce is a mixture of hot, sweet and salty flavours generously laced with ginger and garlic and cooked with vinegar. It is easy to buy both types.

CLOUD EARS

See wood fungus.

CHINESE PARSLEY

See coriander.

COCONUT MILK

Not the water inside the nut, as is commonly believed, but the creamy liquid extracted from the grated flesh of fresh coconuts or from desiccated (shredded) coconut. When coconut milk is called for, do try to use it, for the flavour cannot be duplicated by using any other kind of milk.

CORIANDER

All parts of the coriander plant are used in Asian cooking. The dried seed is the main ingredient in curry powder, and although not hot it has a fragrance that makes it an essential part of a curry blend.

The fresh coriander herb is also called Chinese parsley or cilantro. Although it may take some getting used to because of its pungent smell (the name comes from the Greek *koris*, meaning 'bug'), Southeast Asian food is not the same

without it. It is indispensable in Burma, Thailand, Vietnam, India and China where it is also called 'fragrant green'. If you have difficulty obtaining it, grow fresh coriander yourself in a small patch of garden or even a window box. Scatter the seeds, sprinkle lightly with soil and water every day. They take about 18 days to germinate. Pick them when about 15 cm (6 inches) high and do not allow plants to go to seed.

CUMMIN or CUMIN

Cummin is, with coriander, the most essential ingredient in prepared curry powders. It is available as seed, or ground. There is some confusion between cummin and caraway seeds because they are similar in appearance, but the flavours are completely different and one cannot replace the other in recipes.

DASHI

A clear soup made from dried bonito flakes and seaweed. Instant *dashi*, sold in Japanese stores, is made from *katsuobushi* (powdered dried bonito) and *kombu* (seaweed). It is essential for Japanese cooking, for in addition to being served as a soup it is used as a cooking stock or as part of a dipping sauce.

DRIED SHRIMP PASTE

A pungent paste made from prawns, and used in many Southeast Asian recipes. It is sold in cans or flat slabs or cakes and will keep indefinitely. If stored in a tightly closed jar it will, like a genie in a bottle, perform its magic when required without obtruding on the kitchen at other times! It does not need refrigeration. Commercially sold as 'blachan'.

FISH SAUCE

A thin, salty, brown sauce used in Southeast Asian cooking to bring out the flavour in other foods. A small variety of fish is packed in wooden barrels with salt, and the liquid that runs off is the 'fish sauce'. Substitute light soy sauce, adding to each cup one teaspoon of dried shrimp paste, which has been wrapped in foil and grilled for 5 minutes on each side and then powdered. Stir well and bottle. Shake bottle before use. There are different grades of fish sauce, the Vietnamese version being darker and having a more pronounced fish flavour than the others.

FIVE SPICE POWDER

Essential in Chinese cooking, this reddish brown powder is a combination of ground star anise, fennel, cinnamon, cloves and Szechwan pepper.

GALANGAL, LESSER

Also known as 'aromatic ginger', this member of the ginger family cannot be used as a substitute for ginger or vice versa. It is used only in certain dishes, and gives a pronounced aromatic flavour. When available fresh, it is sliced or pounded to a pulp; but outside of Asia it is usually sold dried, and the hard round slices must be pounded with a mortar and pestle or pulverised in a blender before use. In some spice ranges it is sold in powdered form.

GARAM MASALA

A mixture of ground spices used in Indian cooking. Place each ingredient separately in a dry frying pan and cook for about 2 minutes, stirring constantly: 2 tablespoons whole black peppercorns; 1 tablespoon black caraway seeds; 1 teaspoon whole cloves; 2 teaspoons cardamom seeds; 2 teaspoons fennel seeds. As each one is roasted, turn on to a plate to cool. Put all together into container of electric blender, add 2 small cinnamon sticks, broken into pieces. Cover and blend on high speed until finely ground, or pound with a mortar and pestle. Store in a small airtight glass jar. No substitute.

GINGER

A rhizome with a pungent flavour, it is essential in most Asian dishes. Fresh ginger root should be used: powdered ginger cannot be substituted for fresh ginger, for the flavour is quite different. To prepare for use, scrape off the skin with a sharp knife, and either grate or chop finely (according to recipe requirements) before measuring. To preserve fresh ginger for long periods of time, scrape the skin from the rhizome, divide into sections and pack in a well washed and dried bottle. Pour dry sherry over to completely cover the ginger, cover tightly and store in the refrigerator.

HOI SIN SAUCE

A sweet, spicy, reddish brown sauce of thick pouring consistency made from soy beans, garlic and spices. Used in barbecued pork dishes and as a dip. Keeps indefinitely in a covered jar.

HOT BLACK BEAN SAUCE

Also called 'chilli bean sauce', it is a mixture of fermented soy beans and ground hot chillies. Substitute bean sauce or mashed black beans mixed with Chinese chilli sauce.

KEMIRI NUTS

See candle nut.

KENCUR

See galangal, lesser.

LAOS

A very delicate spice, sold in powder form, *laos* comes from the dried root of the 'greater galangal'. It is so delicate in flavour that it can be omitted from recipes.

LOTUS ROOT

Sometimes available fresh; peel, cut into slices and use as directed. Dried lotus root must be soaked at least 20 minutes in hot water with a little lemon juice added to preserve whiteness. Canned lotus root is readily available, and can be stored in the refrigerator for a few days after being opened.

MIRIN

Japanese rice wine, sweeter than *sake* and used only for cooking. Dry sherry can be substituted.

MUSHROOMS, DRIED CHINESE and JAPANESE

Also known as 'fragrant mushrooms', the flavour of these mushrooms is quite individual. They are expensive but give an incomparable flavour. Soak before using. There is no substitute — dried Continental mushrooms are quite different in flavour.

MUSTARD, BLACK

This variety of mustard seed is smaller and more pungent than the yellow variety. Substitute brown mustard seed (*juncia*). Alba or white mustard is not used in Asian cooking.

OYSTER SAUCE

Adds delicate flavour to all kinds of dishes. Made from oysters cooked in soy sauce and brine, this thick brown sauce can be kept indefinitely without refrigeration.

PALM SUGAR

This strong-flavoured dark sugar is obtained from the sap of coconut palms and Palmyrah palms. The sap is boiled down until it crystallises, and the sugar is usually sold in round, flat cakes or two hemispheres put together to form a ball and wrapped in dried leaves. Substitute black sugar, an unrefined, sticky sugar sold in health food stores, or use refined dark brown sugar sold at supermarkets.

PLUM SAUCE

A spicy, sweet, hot Chinese sauce made from plums, chillies, vinegar, spices and sugar. Use as a dip. It keeps indefinitely in a covered jar.

RICE, FLOUR

A fine textured flour milled from rice, sold at health food stores.

RICE, GROUND

This can be bought at many grocery stores, health food stores and supermarkets, and is slightly more granular than rice flour. It gives a crisp texture when used in batters or other mixtures.

SAMBAL ULEK

A combination of chillies and salt, used in cooking or as an accompaniment. The old Dutch-Indonesian spelling, still seen on some labels, is 'sambal oelek'.

SAKE

Pronounced 'sahk-ay', Japan's famous rice wine is usually served warm — about 44°C (110°F), easily achieved by immersing the wine's container in very hot water for a short time. It is also used as an ingredient in sauces and marinades, when brandy or dry sherry can be substituted.

SESAME SEED

Used mostly in Korean, Chinese and Japanese food, and in sweets in Southeast Asian countries. Black sesame, another variety known as *hak chih mah* (China) or *kuro goma* (Japan), is mainly used in the Chinese dessert, toffee apples, and as a flavouring (*gomasio*) mixed with salt in Japanese food.

SESAME OIL

The sesame oil used in Chinese cooking is extracted from toasted sesame seeds, and gives a totally different flavour from the lighter coloured sesame oil sold in health food stores. For the recipes in this book, buy sesame oil from Chinese stores. Use the oil in small quantities for flavouring, not as a cooking medium.

SESAME PASTE

Sesame seeds, when ground, yield a thick paste similar to peanut butter. Stores specialising in Middle Eastern foods sell a sesame paste known as *tahini*, but this is made from raw sesame seeds, is white and slightly bitter, and cannot be substituted for the Chinese version — which is made from toasted sesame seeds, and is brown and nutty. A suitable substitute is peanut butter with sesame oil added for flavour. Sesame paste is sold in cans or jars, and keeps indefinitely after opening.

SOY SAUCE

Indispensable in Asian cooking, this versatile sauce enhances the flavour of every basic ingredient in a dish. Different grades are available.

Chinese cooking uses light soy and dark soy. The light soy is used with chicken or seafoods, or in soups where the delicate colour of the dish must be retained.

Always use *shoyu* or Japanese soy sauce in Japanese cooking.

In Indonesia, *kecap manis*, a thick, dark, sweetened soy, is often used. As a substitute, use dark Chinese soy with black or brown sugar added in the proportions given in recipes.

All types of soy sauce keep indefinitely without refrigeration.

SPRING ONIONS (SCALLIONS or GREEN ONIONS)

This member of the onion family is known as 'shallot' in Australia, but is correctly called a spring onion almost everywhere else (though the term 'scallion' is popular in the U.S.A.). Spring onions are the thinnings of either *Allium cepa* or *A. fistulum* plantings that do not form a bulb. They are white and slender, with green leaves, and are used widely in China and Japan.

SPRING ROLL WRAPPERS

Thin white sheets of pastry sold in plastic packets and kept frozen. Thaw and peel off one at a time (unused wrappers can be re-frozen). Large wrappers of the *wonton* type cannot be substituted.

STAR ANISE

The dried, star-shaped fruit of an evergreen tree native to China, it consists of 8 segments or points. It is essential in Chinese cooking.

TANGERINE PEEL, DRIED

Sold in Chinese grocery stores, this gives an incomparable flavour to food. Substitute fresh tangerine or mandarin peel, or orange rind.

TURMERIC

A rhizome of the ginger family, turmeric with its orange-yellow colour is a mainstay of commercial curry powders. Though often called Indian saffron, it should never be confused with true saffron and the two may not be used interchangeably.

WALNUTS

Walnuts used in Chinese dishes should be the peeled walnuts sold in Chinese grocery stores, for the thin skin (which turns bitter with cooking) as been removed. If peeled walnuts are not available, use the canned, salted walnuts also sold at Chinese stores: they do not need further cooking. Or pour boiling water over walnut kernels, leave 5 minutes, then peel.

WATER CHESTNUTS

Sometimes available fresh, their brownish black skin must be peeled away with a sharp knife, leaving the crisp, slightly sweet kernel. They are also available in cans, already peeled and in some instances sliced. After opening, store in water in refrigerator for 7-10 days, changing water daily.

WOOD FUNGUS

Also known as 'cloud ear fungus' or 'jelly mushrooms', wood fungus is sold by weight, and in its dry state looks like greyish-black pieces of paper. Soaked in hot water for 10 minutes, it swells to translucent brown shapes like curved clouds or a rather prettily shaped ear — hence the name 'cloud ear fungus'. With its flavourless resilience it is a perfect example of a texture ingredient, adding no taste of its own but takes on subtle flavours from the foods with which it is combined. Cook only for a minute or two.

WONTON WRAPPERS

Small squares of fresh noodle dough available at Chinese grocery stores. They can be refrigerated for up to a week if well wrapped in plastic, or can be wrapped in foil and frozen. Sold by weight, there are approximately 90 wrappers to the half kilogram (one pound).

INDEX

Figures in bold indicate illustration.